the Decorated Bag

embellishing handbags, purses, and totes

Genevieve A. Sterbenz

CREATIVE HOMEOWNER®, Upper Saddle River, New Jersey

COPYRIGHT © 2006

CREATIVE
HOMEOWNER®

A Division of Federal Marketing Corp.
Upper Saddle River, NJ

THE DECORATED BAG

SENIOR EDITOR: Carol Sterbenz
SENIOR DESIGNER: Glee Barre
ASSISTANT EDITOR: Evan Lambert
TECHNICAL EDITOR: Candie Frankel
PHOTO RESEARCHER: Robyn Poplasky
INDEXER: Schroeder Indexing Services
PRINCIPAL PHOTOGRAPHY: Steven Mays
INSTRUCTIONAL PHOTOGRAPHY: Marta and Ben Curry
PATTERNS AND ORIGINAL ART: Marta Curry and Roberta Frauwirth

CREATIVE HOMEOWNER

VP/PUBLISHER: Brian Toolan
VP/EDITORIAL DIRECTOR: Timothy O. Bakke
PRODUCTION MANAGER: Kimberly H. Vivas
ART DIRECTOR: David Geer
MANAGING EDITOR: Fran J. Donegan

Printed in China

Current Printing (last digit)
10 9 8 7 6 5 4 3 2 1

The Decorated Bag, First Edition
Library of Congress Control Number: 2005933624
ISBN-10: 1-58011-296-X
ISBN-13: 978-1-58011-296-3

CREATIVE HOMEOWNER®
A Division of Federal Marketing Corp.
24 Park Way
Upper Saddle River, NJ 07458
www.creativehomeowner.com

dedication

For Frank, who makes my life richer, happier, and better every single day.

Table of Contents

Making Designer Bags

Patterns and Diagrams

Introduction

WITH HIP STYLE and sparkling imagination, *The Decorated Bag* brings the fabulous, must-have accessory, the handbag, within your reach without having to spend a small fortune.

THE DECORATED BAG consists of 26 designs, shown in 175 full-page and up-close color photographs, and accompanied by simple step-by-step instructions. Filled with original designs that feature great fabrics—like faux fur and luxurious velvet—and cool design details—like handles made from gold chains and beaded necklaces—"The Collection" features such fashion faves as a purse paved with rhinestones, an envelope in Tiffany blue suede, a cherry red tote bag with a graphic silhouette, and much, much more. The illustrated glossaries at the end of the work provide an overall look at the featured bags and another 26 style variations.

THE DECORATED BAG will inspire you to create a designer bag, even if you do not consider yourself particularly crafty. All you need to do is add embellishments—such as beads, trim, and anything else that attracts your eye—to a purchased bag. If you wish to sew the popular pull-string, clutch-, saddle-, or envelope-style bags, patterns are included, along with tips for recycling the glam stuff you may already have. *The Decorated Bag* is simply a starting point for you to create the perfect bag for any occasion.

The Collection

Acquiring the most fabulous bag is easy when you create it yourself using your imagination, your great sense of style, and a few sparkling embellishments. "The Collection" will inspire you to make one (or more) for every occasion.

Bejeweled Evening Bag

An ornate brooch, dangling chandelier earrings, and a profusion of crystal beads and pearls decorate this lush green velvet bag, the perfect accessory for an evening out. The secret to the beaded design is the use of costume jewelry and a liberal scattering of sparkling crystal beads. The central brooch, with its dainty forget-me-knots, was once a pendant. Pieces of the necklace chain are used to connect the elements in this jewelry collage.

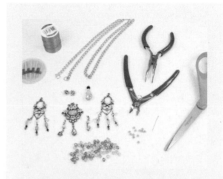

MATERIALS
- Necklace with ornate floral brooch
- 4 chandelier earrings with dangling beads
- 2 pink rhinestone florettes
- 50 green crystal beads, 5mm
- 50 pink crystal beads, 5mm
- 25 mini pink pearls, 4mm
- 1 jewelry head pin, 12" long
- 1 blue crystal teardrop, ⅝" long
- 1 green crystal bead, 6 mm
- 1 red crystal bead, 6mm
- Cotton thread that matches the bag
- 1 yd. gold link chain

TOOLS
- Bent-nose chain pliers
- Wire cutters
- Scissors
- Hand sewing needle

THE FEATURED BAG*
Soft velvet pouch with metal closure, approximately 6½" high x 7" wide x 4" deep

*To make this bag, see page 116.

13

decorating the bejeweled evening bag

1 Separate the brooch from its chain using the bent-nose chain pliers; remove the wire hooks from two chandelier earrings. Following the diagram, position the brooch and earrings on the bag. Tack them in place.

2 Cut a 3-in. length of chain. Secure a 1-in. length between an earring and the brooch, using pliers to open and close the links. Join the free end to make a triangle. Tack it in place. Repeat on the opposite side of the brooch.

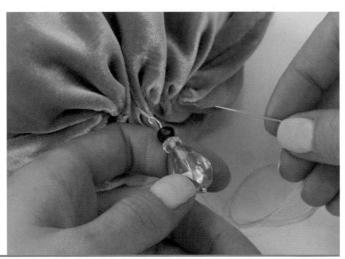

3 Cut beaded lengths from the remaining earrings, and attach them to each point of the chain triangles. Sew the crystal beads and pearls to the bag. Sew pink rhinestone florettes to the centers of the chain triangles.

4 Insert a head pin through the blue crystal teardrop, the green bead, and the red bead. Bend the end of the pin into a loop, using pliers. Tack the loop to the gathered bottom of the bag. Attach the chain strap to each side of the frame at the "V."

beading placement diagram

Beading Placement Key

- ◌ Earrings and Brooch
- ◌ Dangling Ornaments
- X Crystal Beads
- • Mini Pink Pearls
- ▲ Rinestone Florette

Center Line

Earring

Brooch

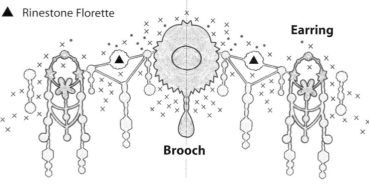

This evening bag takes on a whole new look when made in a red gingham cotton printed with large roses. For surprising glamour, sew on seed beads in matching colors, following the lines and shapes of the motifs printed on the fabric in a "paint by number" fashion. The unadorned cotton bag will be instantly transformed into a showpiece that has sparkle and shine. To add a shoulder strap, attach the ends of a long chain necklace to opposite sides of the purse frame.

design tip

Costume jewelry of exquisite description is available everywhere for very reasonable prices. There may even be several appealing pieces in your jewelry box. Harvest plain chains or strands of pearls for use as straps or handles.

Victorian Straw Tote

Surprising elegance is created when a luxurious fur collar with satin ribbon streamers, meant to dress up a sweater or coat, is married to a simple straw bag and accented with a cameo brooch. The woven straw and chocolate brown fur create a striking contrast in color, texture, and style. Use a collar in a pastel shade for a more subtle look. The same bag can be changed back into a casual day bag in minutes by snipping the tacking threads.

MATERIALS
- Faux fur collar in chocolate brown with satin ribbon ties
- Cotton thread that matches the bag
- Cameo brooch

TOOLS
- Hand sewing needle
- Scissors

THE FEATURED BAG
A straw tote with short handles, measuring approximately 10½" high x 9" wide x 4" deep

17

decorating the victorian straw tote

1 Wrap the faux fur collar around the mouth of the bag.

2 Tie the ribbon ends into a bow, adjusting the tie for a snug fit.

design tip

It is easy to make a decorative fur collar exactly to your liking.

Fabric and trim stores sell faux fur by the yard. Buy a length that is equal to the circumference of your bag, and attach it to your bag as shown.

When you are attaching a fur collar to a bag, use thread in a color that matches the color of the bag, not the color of the fur. The stitches you sew will be hidden within the fur pile on the outside of the bag, but they will be seen on the inside.

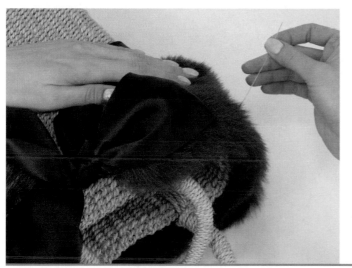

3 Use a threaded needle to sew the collar and the bow to the straw bag, poking the needle between the hairs and pulling the thread tightly until the fur backing lays flat against the straw. Sew all the way around the bag to secure the collar in place.

4 Pin the cameo brooch to the center of the ribbon bow. Hand-stitch the back of the pin to the bag to secure it in place.

variation

A quick and easy makeover for a straw bag is to decorate it with a striped grosgrain ribbon and a silk flower. The ribbon is tied into a bow around the handle, and the stem of the flower is secured to the ribbon with a small safety pin. The best part about this simple accent is that it can be changed in a matter of minutes to coordinate with any new outfit or outing. Consider adding daisies and a yellow ribbon for a summer picnic, or use a pink cabbage rose with a mint green ribbon for a romantic lunch *à deux!*

Big-City Bowling Bag

This faux leather bag, with its fun shape, bubblegum color, and brass accents, is the perfect candidate for an embellishment upgrade! The raised leather details, piping, and stitching form shaped insets on both the front and the back of the bag where pretty fabric can be inlaid. To create a pattern that allows fabric to fit perfectly within the insets, photocopy the actual bag and use the printed copy as a pattern to cut the fabric to size.

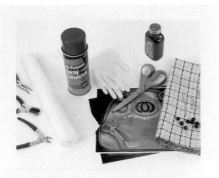

MATERIALS
- ³/₈ yd. plaid fabric, "Chanel-style"
- 2 10" x 12" sheets of rice paper
- 1 yd. gold link chain
- 2 black jet beads, 5mm
- 2 black jet beads, 1cm
- 4 jewelry head pins, 1" long
- Contact cement

TOOLS
- Scissors with straight blades
- Small scissors with curved blades
- Straight pins
- Wire cutter
- Bent-nose chain pliers
- Nylon-jaw pliers
- Pattern
- Latex gloves

THE FEATURED BAG
A sturdy "leather" bag with hinged handles, zip closure, and inset design, approximately 8" high x 10" wide x 3 ³/₄ " deep

21

decorating the big-city bowling bag

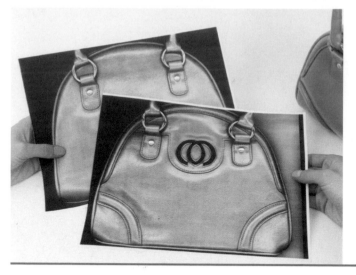

1 Stuff the bag to eliminate any surface wrinkles. Photocopy the front and back of the bag. Label the copies "front" and "back."

2 To make the patterns, mark and cut out the sections of the photocopies that will be replaced by fabric. Lay the cutout sections into the inset areas of the bag to ensure that they fit.

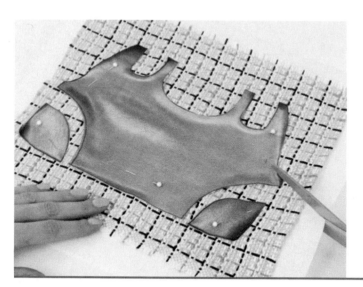

4 Pin the pattern for the front of the bag to the laminated fabric. Cut out each section, following the pattern, using small scissors for curved lines. Remove the pins, and set the fabric sections aside. Repeat to cut the sections for the back of the bag.

5 Lay a center section wrong side up on a protected work surface. Apply a coat of contact cement. Turn the section over, and press it into position, adhering the bottom edges first and working upwards. Repeat until all sections are adhered.

Laminating rice paper to the wrong side of the decorative fabric provides "tooth" so that the fabric adheres better to the bag. It also prevents shifting, which can cause pattern distortion.

3 Cut two 10-in. by 12-in. rectangles of fabric. Put on latex gloves. Apply spray adhesive to the wrong side of the fabric and rice paper. Press the coated sides together to laminate layers.

variation

A simple way to dress up a plain leather bag is to use appliqués. These chic, yet retro, quilted satin pink poodle appliqués seemed the perfect compliment to this pink bowling bag. Although many appliqués have adhesive backs and only require ironing to secure them, the faux leather of this bag would not be able to withstand the heat. The poodle appliqués were applied using contact cement. Follow step 6 to create the chain leashes.

6 Cut a 14- and a 16-in. length of chain using wire cutters. Thread a head pin through each bead. Using both pliers, attach the smaller beads to the shorter chain and the larger beads to the longer chain. Thread the chains through the handle.

Hollywood Hatbox

A '50s style hatbox in black, white, and pink has simple yet stunning glamour girl appeal. Accented with velvet ribbon and a rhinestone belt buckle, it is the perfect carryall for that girl on the go. We started with a super-sturdy hatbox found at a millinery store. After the embellishments were applied to the lid, a ribbon hinge was added to keep the lid and box together. A beaded handle was attached, adding a finishing touch of retro chic.

MATERIALS
- 14" pink velvet ribbon, 2" wide
- 14" black velvet ribbon, $\frac{1}{4}$" wide
- Pink rhinestone belt buckle, $2\frac{1}{4}$" wide
- Beaded handle

TOOLS
- Permanent adhesive
- Scissors

THE FEATURED BAG
A traditional hatbox constructed of paper-covered cardboard, approximately 12" in diameter x 6" deep

25

decorating the hollywood hatbox

1 Place pink ribbon, plush side up, on a flat surface. Lay the black ribbon wrong side up, and apply scant dabs of glue to its length. Hold the black ribbon by the ends, and press it, glue side down, to the length of pink ribbon; let the glue dry.

2 Insert the ribbon through the belt buckle, sliding the buckle to the midpoint of the ribbon. Apply dabs of glue to the underside of the buckle, and adhere it to the ribbon. Let the glue dry.

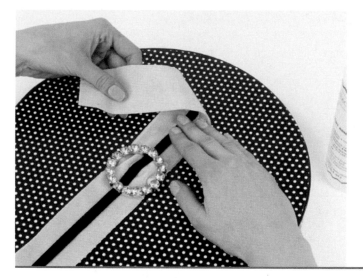

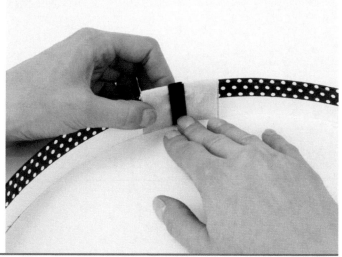

3 Lay the ribbon across the lid of the hatbox, positioning the buckle in the center. Apply dabs of glue to the underside of the ribbon to secure it to the top and sides of the lid.

4 Turn the lid over. Fold the ends of the ribbon to the inside of the lid, and secure it with dabs of glue. Let the glue dry.

To

add a handle to

the hatbox, begin by

removing the cord, which is

threaded through premade grom-

met holes. Use two of the holes to

attach the screw ends of the beaded

handle. Simply insert one screw

through each hole at the outside of the

lid, and secure it on the inside of the

box with a nut. Attach the lid to the

hatbox by creating a hinge from wide

black silk ribbon. Glue the ribbon to

the interior rim of the lid and the

box, opposite the handle. Add a

latch at the opposite side to

secure the lid to the box,

if desired.

variation

Elegant braided appliqués in gold are combined with a three-dimensional monogram and a wide silk ribbon handle. The monogram is made from a wooden letter that is painted gold. The monogram and the appliqués are affixed to the hatbox using permanent adhesive. The soft, shimmering handle is a 2½ - in. wide silk variegated ribbon in gold. Small gold beads anchor the handle as a finishing touch.

"Miss Kitty" Tote

Graphically striking and whimsical, this "Miss Kitty" tote started out as a plain felted wool bag with leather accents and blanket stitch embroidery. Unfortunately, it also had a stain that wouldn't come out. To salvage the tote, a cat appliqué was added. Cut from black felt, the sleek kitty motif was glued to the front of the bag, and then bejeweled using a few rhinestone accents harvested from a piece of sparkling costume jewelry.

MATERIALS
- ¼ yd. black wool felt
- Black and silver rhinestones from a bracelet, or costume jewelry, as desired

TOOLS
- Pattern (page 132)
- Scissors
- Straight pins
- Fabric glue
- Permanent adhesive
- Tweezers

THE FEATURED BAG
A sturdy felted wool tote with leather handles, approximately 13" high x 18" wide at the mouth x 12" wide at the base x 5" deep

29

decorating the "miss kitty" tote

1 Enlarge the pattern on page 132 using a photocopier. Make several copies, sizing the image to fit the bag front. Cut out the pattern on the marked outline.

2 Lay the wool felt on a flat surface. Place the pattern on top, and secure the layers with straight pins. Cut along the edge of the pattern to make the felt appliqué.

variation

Key chains are among the most abundant sources for accenting your tote bag. Available in an inexhaustible variety of materials and themes, key chains can be used to add sparkle, wit, style, and personality to any tote.

This cute little key chain is made up of a cluster of hand crocheted flowers and beads that dangle in a bouquet shape. Its lobster-claw closure allows it to hook securely to the leather handle of the tote.

To make a decorated key chain of your own design, clip a lobster-claw finding to a large split ring. Then thread on a collection of charms, souvenirs, or even dazzling, over-the-top costume jewelry. When you are happy with your design, use the lobster claw to attach the decoration to the handle of your tote bag.

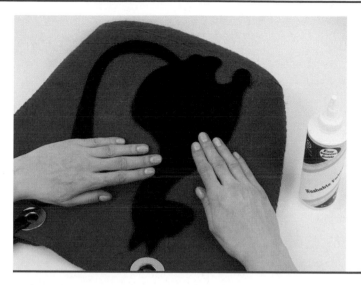

3 Lay the tote bag flat on a flat work surface. Apply an even film of glue to the wrong side of the cut appliqué. Place the appliqué glue side down on the tote. Press to adhere it.

4 Grasp a rhinestone with tweezers, and apply a dab of glue to its back . Press the rhinestone to the neck of the cat. Continue to add rhinestones, alternating colors, to form a collar.

sources for motifs

A good source of line art for simple graphic shapes is a child's coloring book. The drawings are outlined in heavy black line, making them easy to convert to simple silhouettes. Use a copier to make several images, sizing them differently so that you can fit the drawing to the space you wish to decorate. You can arrange images of flowers, animals, and other decorative motifs indepently or in a group on your bag. You can place them on one side of the bag in a pleasing array, or you can use them to decorate both sides of the bag, if you prefer. The appliqué is the same as shown.

design tip

Felted wool is particulary suited to making decorative appliqués. It is easy to cut and its edges do not ravel. Felted wool comes in a variety of sophisticated colors. Consider arranging daisy appliqués, each in a different pastel color, on a tote made from felted wool in the very softest leaf green.

American Beauty Bag

Found casually tossed on a yard sale table, this beautiful rose-covered clutch was once a worn little bag—possibly abandoned by a bridesmaid. Its structure and fabric were intact, providing a sound foundation for the ribbon "rose" decoration applied to its sides. Each ribbon rose is made from a length of folded ribbon and tacked in place on the bag until all the fabric is concealed. A necklace handle provides a delicate finishing touch.

MATERIALS
- Silk ribbon in red, 2½" wide (Shown: Hanah Silk ribbon in American Beauty)
- Thread in red
- 60 pearls in ivory, 4mm
- Chain necklace, 13½" long

TOOLS
- Scissors
- Hand sewing needle
- Bent-nose chain pliers

THE FEATURED BAG
An elongated softly structured rectangle with a snap closure approximately 4" high x 8½" wide at the top and 10" wide at the bottom x 3" deep

decorating the american beauty bag

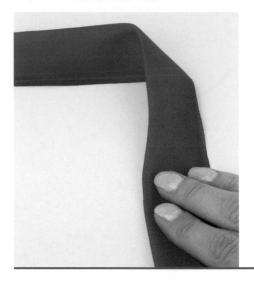 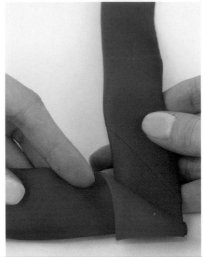 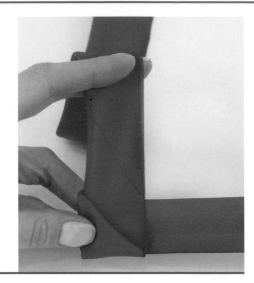

1 Cut a 20-in. length of ribbon, and fold it in half. Lay it horizontally on a flat surface. At its midpoint, fold the right-hand streamer down to create a right angle.

2, 3 Fold the same right streamer under the ribbon as shown, bringing the streamer up. Fold and tuck the left streamer under the folds and to the right. Fold and tuck the "up" streamer under the folds and down. Fold and tuck the right streamer under the folds and to the left. Repeat steps 2–3 five times.

 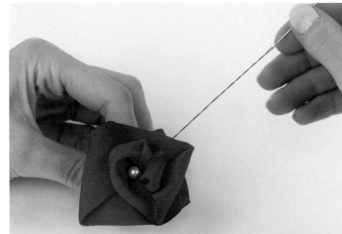

5 Wind and tie a thread around the streamers, close to the base of the "rose," to secure the rose shape.

6 Use a threaded needle to sew back and forth through the center of a rose to secure it. Before cutting off the threaded needle, sew one pearl to the center of the rose, ending with tiny stitches at the back.

For a fun and sophisticated look, use tassel trim to decorate your bag. Simply glue on lengths of trim in an overlapping pattern. Begin by folding under the cut ends of the trim. Then pin and glue the braided edge to the bag. When applying subsequent lengths, butt the braided edges against each other so that the hanging tassels overlap.

4 Hold the base of the folds, and let the ribbon pop out. Still holding the short ribbon streamers, pull one through your hand, allowing the ribbon folds to gather into a rose shape.

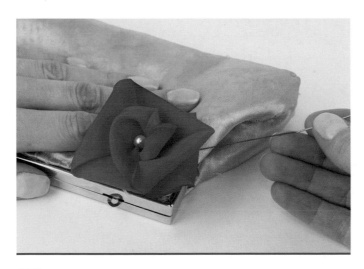

7 Snip off the loose streamers. Hand-stitch the rose to the bag. Repeat steps 1–6 to make enough roses to cover the bag. To add a chain handle, use the pliers to secure one jump ring to each end of the necklace and the existing hardware on the bag.

design tip

To eliminate waste, unspool 18 inches of ribbon but do not cut the ribbon off the roll. Choose a midpoint, and follow steps 1–4, pulling the streamer attached to the roll to form the rose. Then cut the ribbon.

Mod Print Tote

Flash back to the '60s with this Mod Print Tote accented with sequins. The pink-and-white floral pattern lends a Pucci-style swirl of color. Simply fill in the design contours with the chosen embellishment. For a bold effect, let the rich black outline of the design show through. For a more subtle look, apply clear iridescent sequins over the black lines to quiet the color without losing the sparkle.

MATERIALS
- 1 bag (1,000 pieces) mint green flat sequins, 5mm
- 1 bag (1,000 pieces) pale crystal iridescent flat sequins, 5mm
- 1 bag (1,000 pieces) hot pink flat sequins, 5mm
- Permanent embellishing glue

TOOLS
- Tweezers

THE FEATURED BAG
A printed fabric bag with side pleats, a front zip pocket, and short shoulder straps, approximately 11" high x 16" wide x 6" deep

decorating the mod print tote

1 Lay the bag, front side up, on a clean work surface. Choose one color area within the printed pattern on which to work. Here, green was selected. Empty the color-coordinated sequins into a small dish. Pick up one sequin with tweezers and apply embellishing glue to the back.

2 Turn over the sequin, and press it in place, glue side down, within the confines of one green area bounded by black lines. Repeat until the selected area is covered. Overlap the sequins for a denser effect, if desired.

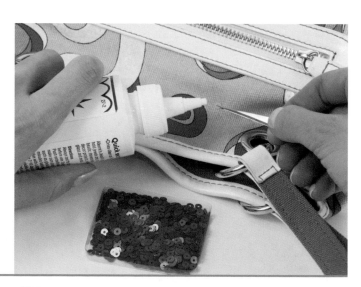

4 Follow steps 1-3 to apply crystal sequins to all the white areas on the bag.

5 Follow steps 1-3 to apply pink sequins to the dark pink areas on the bag.

3 Repeat steps 1 and 2 to apply sequins to the remaining green areas on the front of the bag.

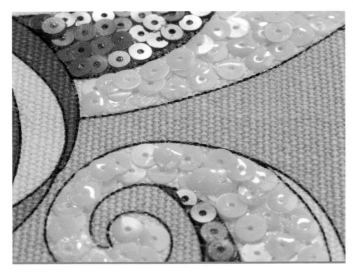

6 To decorate the other side of the bag, turn the bag over, and repeat steps 1-5.

design tip

Sequins may loosen up with everyday wear and tear. You can repair and replace loose and missing sequins, or simply leave one side unadorned.

variation

Vintage clip-on earrings are the perfect "find," adding color and dimension to the center of these flower bursts. While jewelry boxes and drawers may be great immediate sources of costume jewelry, do not overlook the potential of thrift shops and garage sales for unique pieces. Finding pairs of earrings is not necessary. Look for one-of-a-kind items that are similar in style or color.

Blue Suede Portfolio

A *small touch of color can add a lot of style to any bag. Here, a sleek folio in robin's egg blue is accented by a narrow stripe in canary yellow. Cut from faux suede, the stripe delineates the flap and adds cheerful elegance.*

MATERIALS
- *Scrap of yellow faux suede*
- *Contact cement in a bottle containing a brush*

TOOLS
- *Rotary cutter*
- *Self-healing mat*
- *Ruler*

THE FEATURED BAG*
An envelope- or folio-style bag in laminated faux suede, approximately 11" high x 13" wide

*To make this bag, see page 118.

making the accent stripe

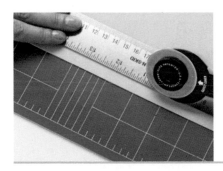

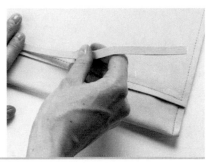

1. Measure and cut a ³/₈-in.-wide by-14-in.-long strip of faux suede, using the ruler and the rotary cutter.

2. Apply a coat of cement to one side of the strip. Position and press the strip, glue side down, to the flap.

Tropical Demi

A decorative pin or brooch dresses up any handbag—creating instant style. While brooches are available in a wide variety of shapes and sizes, they also tend to be expensive. To get the look of a sparkling brooch without spending a bundle, transform a decorative accent into a pin. Here, a pin-back was added to a sequined orange flower. The flower was pinned, along with some leaves, to a plain demi-style bag, introducing colorful contrast.

MATERIALS
- Sequined orange flower
- Pin back
- Sequined green leaf pin
- Thread in orange and green

TOOLS
- Hand sewing needle
- Scissor

THE FEATURED BAG
A soft leather bag with zip closure and shoulder strap, approximately 4½" high x 10" wide x 3" deep

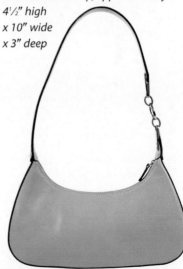

decorating the tropical demi

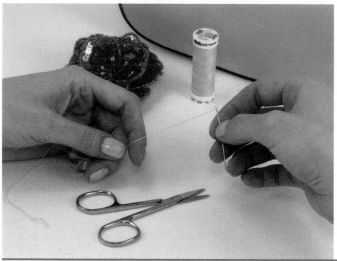

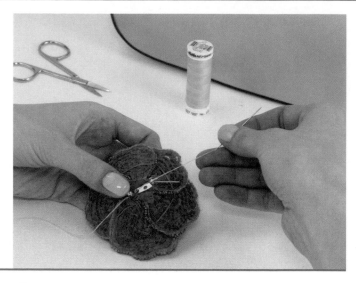

1 Thread a sewing needle with thread that coordinates with the flower, doubling the thread and knotting the ends together.

2 Turn the flower over, and hold the open pinback against it with your thumb. Sew small stitches to trap the flat bar against the flower back.

4 Check the back of the leaf pin. If the existing pinback is not securely attached, remove it and repeat steps 1–3 to sew a pinback in place.

5 Position and pin the leaf cluster to the bag as shown.

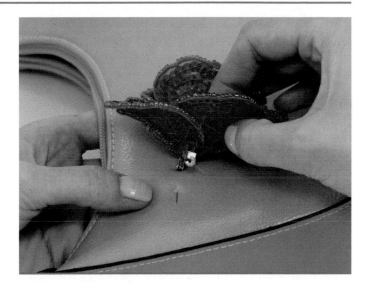

3 Select a spot to place the flower on the bag. Open the bag, and slip one hand inside, palm side up. Use the opposite hand to carefully push the pin down and through the leather until it exits the bag in the desired position; lock the pinback.

6 Use a needle with matching thread to tack the back petals of the flower and leaf pin to the bag. Make small stitches.

variation

Another attractive possibility for adding a simple decoration to a bag is an appliqué. Available in every conceivable motif, appliqués are usually beaded, embroidered, painted, or treated to some kind of elaborate surface decoration. Appliqués have flat backs, making them easy to attach to handbags with smooth surfaces. Here, an oversized rose appliqué covered in pink, sage, cream, and white sequins adds a bold yet softly toned shape to the front of the featured bag.

design tip

A smart way to hide any stains or worn areas on a leather bag is to add one or more decorative pins.

Blue-Boots Tote

T his cute cowgirl in oversized boots is an original illustration printed onto fabric. The easy "T-shirt" transfer technique uses photo transfer paper and a household iron. It allows you to make a transfer print of any image. Use your computer to scan the chosen image, flip it to create a mirror image, and print the image on transfer paper. The image can be adhered to any flat, tightly woven fabric. Here, colorful ribbons and lace frame the image.

MATERIALS
- 1 sheet of T-shirt transfer paper
- ¼ yd. cotton fabric with flat weave in white or pale pastel
- Matching thread
- 1 yd. multicolored trim, ¾" wide
- 1¼ yds. striped ribbon in red and white, ⅝" wide
- 1½ yds. lace trim in red, ¾" wide
- Spray adhesive
- Permanent adhesive

TOOLS
- Art (page 133)
- Ruler
- Scissors
- Straight pins
- Iron
- Sewing machine
- Press cloth
- Computer and scanner

THE FEATURED BAG
A patchwork-style cloth tote with softly structured sides and two short carry handles, approximately 17" high x 15" wide x 6" deep

decorating the blue-boots tote

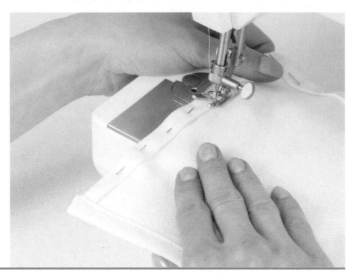

1 Scan the artwork into the computer. Resize the image to fit within an 8-by-10-in. frame. Flip the picture to create a mirror image. Print it to the transfer paper. Trim close to the image.

2 Iron the cotton fabric flat. Cut an 8¼-in.-by-10¼-in. rectangle. Fold in each edge ¼ in., press, and pin. Machine stitch ⅛ in. from the edge all around, removing the pins as you work.

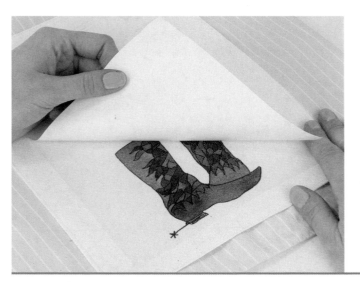

4 Let the transfer image cool. Peel up the paper backing to reveal the image transferred to the cotton rectangle.

5 Lay the transfer on a protected work surface, wrong side up. Spray on an even coat of adhesive. Position and press the transfer to the center of the bag, glue side down, smoothing it with your hands to adhere.

3 Place the press cloth on the ironing board, laying the hemmed rectangle right side up on top. Center the transfer, image side down. Use a hot, dry iron to adhere the image.

6 Cut four lengths of multi-colored trim to "frame" the cotton panel. Secure the trim using permanent adhesive. Repeat to add the striped ribbon and the red lace trim.

design tip

Personalize a cloth diaper bag for a new mother by adding a photo transfer of the newborn baby or images found on baby gift wrap and greeting cards.

variation

Charms are such a fun way to decorate a bag. They come in a great variety of themes, sizes, and finishes, so finding just the right ones to personalize a bag is easy. Simply use a hand sewing needle and thread to match your bag to tack charms in place, arranging them in a pleasing way.

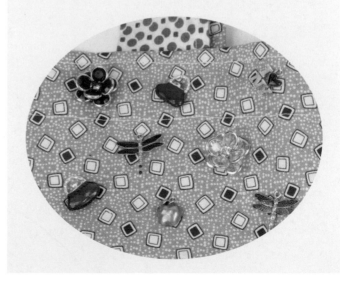

Buttoned-Up Hobo Bag

The hand-knit cables that form the foundation of this cool bag can barely be seen through all the buttons and beads that cover its sides. Adorned with red, orange, and pink buttons and beads in every conceivable size and shape, the sassy decorative effect is super-simple to achieve. Find your own hidden treasure in local thrift shops and trimming and sewing stores. Vintage and one-of-a-kind beads and buttons are perfect for this chic collage.

MATERIALS
- 150 buttons in assorted shades of red
- 100 round beads in cherry red:
  - 50, ¾" wide
  - 50, 1cm wide
- Red thread

TOOLS
- Hand sewing needle
- Scissors

THE FEATURED BAG
A knitted bag lined in satin and accented with a pair of black leather handles, approximately 11" high x 14" wide x 8" deep

decorating the buttoned-up hobo bag

1 Use a threaded needle to sew one-half of the beads to the front of the bag, one at a time, using two or three tiny stitches at the back of each bead to anchor it before continuing to add more. Create an overall pattern, concentrating the larger beads on the lower third of the bag.

2 Sew one-half of the buttons to the bag front, one at a time, once again anchoring each button with two or three tiny stitches. Intermix the buttons and the beads, concentrating the larger buttons on the bottom third of the bag.

design tip

*Buttons
and beads add weight to the bag. To prevent a knit bag
from sagging, be sure it has a lining. Tack the lining to the bag with
needle and thread in strategic places whenever the added weight of the decoration
is causing distortion. To lighten the bag without sacrificing the look,
add fewer buttons and beads or decorate
only one side of the bag.*

3 Continue to sew on buttons, filling the wider gaps with larger buttons and the narrow spaces with the smaller buttons, until the desired effect is achieved.

4 Repeat steps 1–3 to decorate the other side of the bag, using the remaining buttons and beads.

variation

Pom-poms make great accent decorations. They are so popular that they can be seen in stores and boutiques everywhere. Single pom-poms dangle from hats and mittens. Clusters decorate sweaters and scarves. Here, the featured knitted bag is transformed by a covering of plump pom-poms in red, lending cozy texture and chic style. Pom-poms are so easy to make, you may want to create some of your own. All that is required is yarn, a darning needle, scissors, and a credit card. The credit card is an instant tool around which the yarn is wound, forming loops that make up the pom-pom. To make one pom-pom or many, see the easy steps featured on pages 54 and 55.

making the pom-poms

1 To make one pom-pom, leave a 5-in. tail and wind the yarn around the credit card approximately 50 times.

2 Cut off the excess yarn, leaving a second 5-in. tail. Gently slide the yarn skein off the credit card.

4 Sew the skeins together using a needle threaded with yarn, stitching back and forth through their centers. Pull off the needle. Do not cut the long strands.

5 Hold the sewn skeins, and cut through the loops of yarn, using scissors, to form a scraggly pom-pom. Snip off all but two long strands of yarn.

3 Cut an 8-in. length of yarn and use it to tie the skein at its center, wrapping the yarn around twice and tying a double-knot to secure it. Repeat steps 1–3 to make one more pom-pom.

6 Shake the pom-pom to free the strands. Use scissors to trim and shape the pom-pom into a neat, round ball.

pom-poms

Pom-poms add flirty fun to any bag. They can be used as a single accent, or they can be used to decorate the entire surface of the bag.

To make one plump pom-pom, you will need a ball of yarn, a stiff card like a credit card*, a darning needle or a needle with a big hole and a blunt tip, and scissors.

*Note: The larger the width of the card, the larger the diameter of the pom-pom.

Swingtime Shoulder Bag

The beautiful texture and pattern intrinsic to this crocheted black bag are enhanced by subtle embellishments in the same basic black. Authentic jet beads, rescued from a broken necklace, add a touch of shimmer and shine. Along the bottom edge, swingy tassels add movement. The tassels have an elegant braided detailing that resembles the thread used to crochet the bag. Long fringe and beaded trim could also be used.

MATERIALS
- 54 jet beads, 1cm wide
- 8 tassels in black, 4" long
- Black thread

TOOLS
- Scissors
- Hand sewing needle
- Straight pins
- Adjustable seam gauge

THE FEATURED BAG
A soft, lined, crocheted bag with a pronounced woven texture and short carry handles, approximately 9½" high x 9" wide x 3" deep

decorating the swingtime shoulder bag

1 Lay the bag on a flat work surface. Arrange 23 of the jet beads in five alternating rows of five and four beads each.

2 Mark the position of each bead with a straight pin. Hand-sew each bead to the bag, and remove its marker pin. Repeat to add beads to the opposite side of the bag.

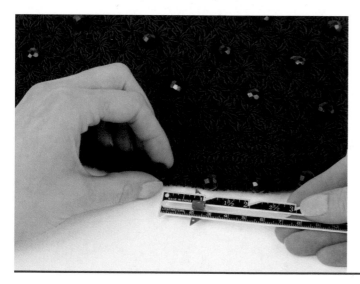

3 Space eight beads along the bottom edge of the bag using the adjustable seam gauge to ensure even intervals. Use a threaded needle to stitch each bead in place.

4 Slip the loop of one tassel over a bottom bead. Sew the loop together to secure the tassel. Repeat to attach the remaining seven tassels.

variation

The wonderful texture and hand-made elegance of this crocheted bag is perfectly complemented by multiple layers of antique cotton lace. Secured to the lower portion of the bag using permanent adhesive, the trim is made up of four lengths of two different trims. Two narrow lengths of mustard yellow lace are bordered by multicolored lace trim in moss green and mustard with some metallic threads added in for shine. The beads and tassels are omitted. For another look, add an extra-wide band of beaded trim in a saturated color like cardinal red. Trim is available in widths from 1 inch to 6 inches. To this extra-wide trim, add a tassel trim. You will find that the decorations will move as the bag is worn.

design tip

This attractive monochromatic bag, ideal for both daytime and evening, features stylish tassels that are typically found in home decorating stores. When searching for creative ideas to embellish any bag, keep in mind that home decorating trends may be a surprising source for inspiration.

Lush Leopard Hatbox

This hatbox-style handbag was originally a cosmetics case repurposed to this sassy little accessory. Decorated with an oversized "rose" made from delicate silk ribbon tinged in brown, the bloom is accented with silk leaves. The decoration has a restrained elegance, while the leopard print fabric introduces wild flair. Buy a rose like this one, or follow the directions on page 32 to make a ribbon rose of your own design, adding the leaves detailed here.

MATERIALS
- Purchased oversized ribbon rose in cream, or one made as on page 32
- Silk ribbon in moss green, $2\frac{1}{2}$" wide
- Thread in green
- Green floral wire, 26 gauge

TOOLS
- Water-soluble fabric pencil in white
- Straight pins
- Sewing machine
- Scissors
- Wire cutter
- Hand sewing needle

THE FEATURED BAG
A structured, fabric-covered hatbox with a hinged lid and handle, approximately 7" high x 8" wide x 4" deep

61

decorating the lush leopard hatbox

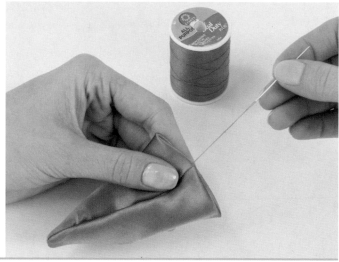

1 Cut two 5½-in. lengths of ribbon. Set one length aside. Lay the other length on a flat surface. Use a fabric pencil to mark a dashed line in a V-shape at one end as shown.

2 Lay the marked ribbon over the second length of ribbon, with all edges even, and secure them with pins. Machine-stitch the sides of the ribbons, followed by the marked V-shape at the leaf top.

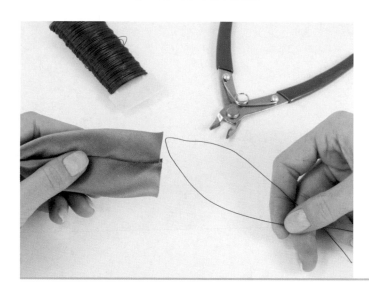

4 Cut an 11-in. length of wire. Fold it in half, and insert the folded end into the leaf opening, allowing the wires to splay apart. Snip off the protruding ends of wire using the wire cutters.

5 Fold under a narrow hem at the raw edge of the ribbon, pressing it down with your fingers. Bring the opposite corners to the center sewing line, and use a threaded needle to tack down the folds.

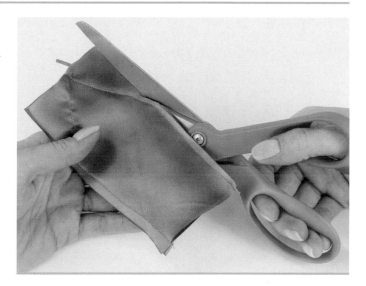

3 Trim away the excess ribbon at the stitched V-shape. Turn the leaf right side out, adjusting the sewn seams so that they run along the middle of the leaf.

6 Repeat steps 1–5 to make two more leaves. When finished, sew them to the back of a ribbon rose so that their ends extend beyond the rose petals. Attach a pin back to the back of the rose, and pin it to the bag. Or use glue to secure it to the bag.

Urban Cowgirl Saddle Bag

A pplying an appliqué to a plain bag can lend extra texture and style. Here, the top flap of an orange saddle bag shows off a surprisingly curvaceous appliqué made of beads, a perfect contrast to the rows of fringe.

MATERIALS
- Beaded appliqué, 8" high x 6½" wide, or as desired
- Contact cement in a bottle containing a brush

THE FEATURED BAG*
A long envelope-style bag with a top flap and a fringed bottom section, approximately
15" high x 10" wide x 6" wide at the opening

*To make this bag, see page 120.

adding the appliqué

1 Use the brush in the bottle to apply a neat, thin coat of cement to the wrong side of the appliqué.

2 Center and press the appliqué, glue side down, to the flap of the bag as shown, or as desired.

Girly Weekender

Whether you're off on a beach excursion, a shopping trip, or a weekend getaway, this hot pink tote makes the perfect carryall. Roomy enough for the essentials and more, the bag is decorated with a lively variety of grosgrain ribbons. Stripes and polka dots in a profusion of colors form parallel stripes across the bottom third of the bag. Grosgrain ribbon is a practical choice because it is tough enough to hold up to everyday wear and tear.

MATERIALS
- Grosgrain ribbon, 9 assorted 1½-yd. lengths, ⅜"–1½" wide
- Thread in matching colors
- Permanent adhesive

TOOLS
- Scissors
- Ruler
- Adjustable seam gauge
- Pencil
- Seam ripper
- Sewing machine

THE FEATURED BAG
A wide tote with a top zipper and carry handles in a hard-working microfiber, approximately 14½" high x 23" wide x 7" deep

making the girly weekender

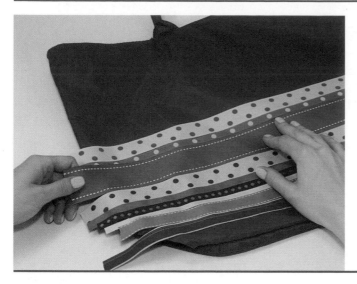

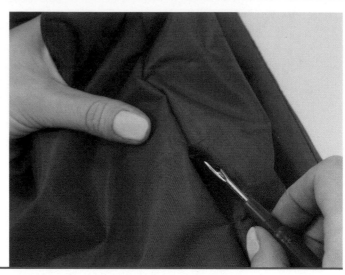

1 Lay the bag on a flat surface. Cut each ribbon in half, making two groups. Lay one group of ribbons horizontally across the bottom of the bag.

2 Mark the ribbon location on the bag. Remove the ribbons, and set them aside. Use a seam ripper to open the side seams of the bag between the marks.

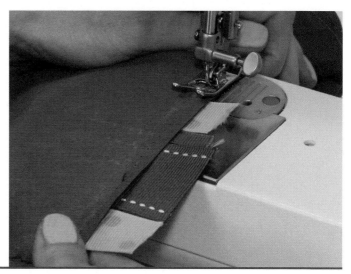

4 Machine-stitch along the edges of each ribbon, beginning at the topmost ribbon and moving down. Repeat steps 3 and 4 to sew the second group of ribbons to the back.

5 Turn the bag wrong side out, and match the ribbon sections at each side. Machine-stitch to close the side seams of the bag. Trim away excess ribbon even with the raw edge of the bag.

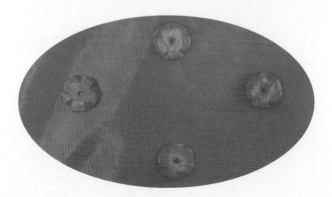

3 Reposition the ribbons on the bag front between the marks, allowing a 2-in. overhang at each side. Glue each ribbon in place, using a ruler to keep the edges parallel. Let the glue dry.

design tip

This closeup view along the side shows the alignment of the ribbon sections' seam. The key to matching up the ribbon sections is careful, accurate gluing in step 3. Complete one side of the bag first. Then use it to guide the placement of the ribbons on the opposite side, for a professional finish.

variation

Pink plastic florettes were removed from a piece of inexpensive costume jewelry, glued onto the tote, and then reinforced with small hand stitches. These florettes proved to be a pretty and practical choice because they are as sturdy and waterproof as the Girly Weekender bag itself.

Springtime Pull-String Bag

Pretty and practical, this polka-dot bag can be opened and closed by pulling on the decorative ribbon at the top of the pouch. Daisy appliqués and little tassels add flirty fun. The appliqués are the iron-on variety and are easy to affix using a hot iron. The tassels at the bottom edge of the bag are made from pink yarn, carrying out the overall springlike feel of the bag. For extra accent, add tassels to the ends of each of the ribbon streamers.

MATERIALS
- 20 daisy appliqués, 1½" wide
- Yarn in pink
- Thread in coordinated colors

TOOLS
- Household iron
- Ironing board
- Ruler, 1½" wide
- Scissors
- Hand sewing needle

THE FEATURED BAG*
A sturdy cotton pouch with a pull-string closure, approximately 8½" high x 9" wide

*To make this bag, see page 124.

decorating the springtime pull-string bag

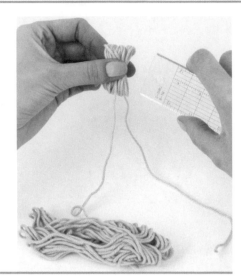

1 Place the daisy appliqués, adhesive side down, on the bag. Fuse them in place using a hot, dry iron.

2 To make one tassel, leave a 3-in. tail of yarn and wind the yarn around the ruler approximately 20 times.

3 Cut off the excess yarn, leaving a second 3-in. tail. Slide the yarn off the ruler.

5 Hold the tassel at the knot. Cut the loops of yarn at the opposite end using scissors.

6 Cut a 5-in. length of yarn from the skein. Lay it flat on the work surface in a horizontal orientation. Position the tassel over the yarn so that only one-fourth of the tassel is above the line of yarn. Bring up both ends of the yarn. Tie a double knot.

4 Place the yarn on a flat surface in the shape of an "O." Cut a 6-in. length of yarn from the skein. Thread the yarn through the center of the "O," exiting the opposite side. Tie a double knot.

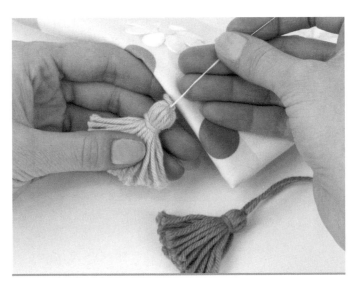

7 Repeat steps 2–6 to make four more tassels. Use a needle and thread to stitch the tassels to the bottom seam of the bag at even intervals, tucking the tails into the tassels.

variation

This pull-string bag was made in pale pink velvet and lined in cotton with a geometric pattern. The white silk rose was attached to the front of the bag for added elegance and flair.

design tip

Pull-string bags can be made in any size. Make several roomy enough for lingerie, shoes, or cosmetics. Or make them to give as party favors or small sentimental gifts.

Snow-Flurry Lipstick Purse

This dazzling purse made from a silver lipstick case is encrusted in glass beads, creating a unique and eyecatching accessory. A super-strong double stick tape designed for crafting is applied to the metal case. The tape is available in rolls and sheets that can be cut to fit any flat suface. Its tack is so strong that it secures the layer of tiny glass beads, which do not have any holes, allowing their polished surfaces to sparkle and glow.

MATERIALS
- 1 sheet double-stick clear plastic with super-tack, 8½" x 11" (Ultimate Bond)
- 1 roll of tape, double-stick clear plastic with super-tack, ⅛" wide (Ultimate Bond)
- 1 2-oz. pkg. no-hole beads, 1mm, in silver

TOOLS
- Black marker
- Scissors
- Decoupage scissors
- Tweezers
- Glass bowl

THE FEATURED CASE
A metal lipstick case in silver tone with an enameled lid on a hinge, approximately 3" high x 8½" wide x 3" deep

decorating the snow-flurry lipstick purse

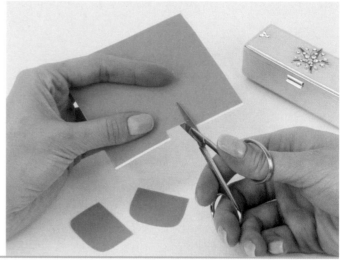

1 Place the sheet, white side up, on a work surface. Position and trace around the short end of the lipstick case, using a black marker. Cut out the marked shape. Repeat at the opposite short end.

2 From the sheet, cut out a rectangle that is slightly larger than 8½ in. by 9½ in. Lay it on the work surface. Wrap the rectangle around the base of the case, allowing it to cover the two long sides and the bottom. Trim the plastic to fit.

variation

The top of the finished purse is embellished with tiny clear rhinestones, which are glued along the edges of four sides of the lid using a permanent beading adhesive. Pink rhinestones are added for a little burst of bright color, breaking the otherwise monochromatic color scheme.

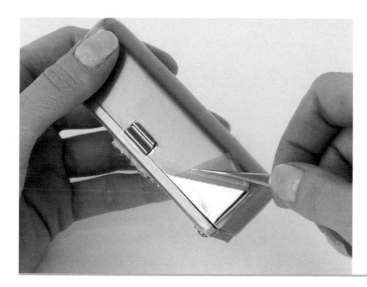

*Another
way to apply the
beads is by sections. Tape all
of the surfaces as described. Then
remove one protective sheet from
each section as you bead. Press
each section into the beads for
best adhesion and
coverage.*

3 Press the tape along the side edges of the lid without removing the pink plastic layer. Remove the white paper from the sections cut in steps 1 and 2, and press them to the case, leaving on the pink protective plastic.

4 Remove the pink protective sheet from all of the sections of tape, exposing the high tack surfaces. Set out a clean container.

5 Carefully hold the case over the container, and pour the beads directly from the package over the exposed tape. Then roll the case in the beads, pressing down firmly on each side to ensure better adhesion and coverage.

SNOW-FLURRY LIPSTICK PURSE 77

Vintage Rhinestone Purse

You never know when you are going to come across a great find. Here, a vintage purse with an etched handle and gorgeous clasp was found on a street vendor's table. In good shape and with beautiful lines, its silk fabric has a geometric design that serves as a ready-made pattern. For a fun look, light rose crystal rhinestones emphasize the pattern, and retro-feel rosettes outline the softly curving top edge of the bag.

MATERIALS
- Approx. 100 crystals* in light rose, 2.5mm
- ½ yd. sequin rosettes in hot pink
- Jewelry glue
  *Or 1 pkg. Swarovski crystals, size SS-10

TOOLS
- Small tray or bowl
- Tweezers
- Decoupage scissors
- Tape measure

THE FEATURED BAG
Boxy purse with plastic handle and snap closure, approximately 4½" high x 8" wide x 2½" deep

decorating the vintage rhinestone purse

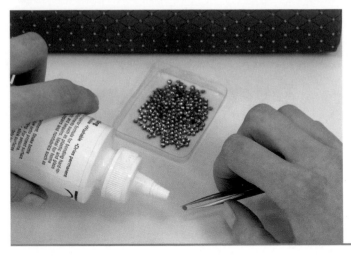

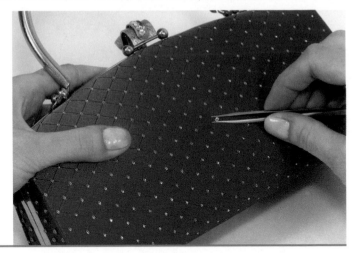

1 Pour the rhinestones into the tray. Using a tweezer, pick up one rhinestone, and turn it to its flat side. Apply a small dab of glue to the center area.

2 Carefully turn the rhinestone over so that the glue side is facing down; then position and lay the rhinestone on the bag, as desired. Gently press down on the rhinestone using the tweezers.

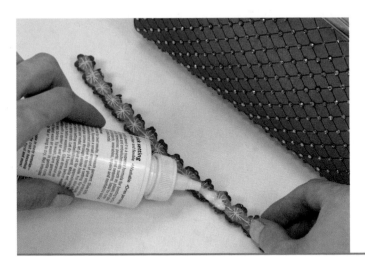

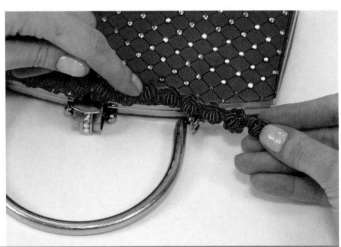

4 Measure and cut two lengths of rosette trim equal in length to the top width of the bag. Lay one length on a flat surface, wrong side up, and carefully apply a thin line of glue.

5 Position one end of the trim at one end of the top of the bag front. Gently press down the trim with your fingers, working across the top curve of the bag. Let the glue dry.

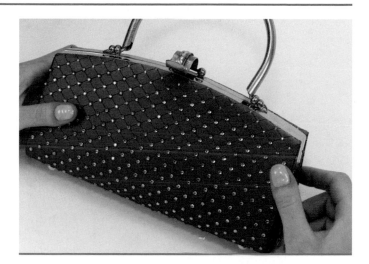

3 Continue to add the rhinestones to the front, back, and sides of the bag following the pattern, or as desired. Leave a ½-in. border at the front and back curves of the bag for the rosette trim. Let the glue dry.

6 Repeat step 5 to apply the rosette trim to the opposite side of the bag. Be careful to avoid getting extra glue on the fabric or on the applied rhinestones. Let the glue dry.

Decorating a bag using elements that reflect your personal style is easy. Here, a Victorian-style necklace with a brooch pendant was used to accent the clasp section of the featured bag, adding enhanced romantic style. To permanently add pieces of jewelry to a cloth bag, first use dabs of glue to affix the pieces; then use a threaded needle to sew tiny whip stitches around jump rings, chains, and other details.

design tip

Try hot-fix rhinestones with adhesive backs. They are easy to apply with a special heating tool and there's no glue mess.

Folk Art Bucket Bag

Made from the softest cashmere blend, this bag puts Old World spin on modern style. The bucket-style bag is decorated with traditional folk motifs—hearts, roses, leaves, and scrollwork. Each element is an individually embroidered appliqué that is either fused or glued in place on the bag. Here, the assortment of motifs is arranged in a symmetrical pattern, but it can also be arranged randomly in an array of pretty design elements.

MATERIALS
- 14 embroidered appliqués with or without adhesive backing:
  - 3 hearts in green with floral details, 1½" high x 1¾" wide
  - 2 scrollwork designs in white, 5" high x 1" wide
  - 2 scrollwork designs in white, 5" high x 3" wide
  - 7 roses in red, 2½" high x 1½" wide
- Optional: permanent adhesive (for use with appliqués without adhesive backing)

TOOLS
- Layout diagram (page 133)
- Household iron
- Tweezers

THE FEATURED BAG
A soft, slouchy bag with a structured bottom, a wide top cuff and a cropped shoulder strap, approximately 11" high x 9" wide x 4" deep

decorating the folk art bucket bag

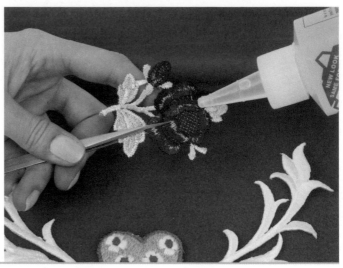

1 Lay two heart appliqués in the center, inverting one over the other. Lay one 1-in.-wide scrollwork appliqué at each side. Continue applying the appliqués, referring to the layout diagram on page 133. Use a hot, dry iron to affix each appliqué.

2 Use permanent adhesive to attach the appliqués that do not have a fusible backing. Place a rose appliqué above the top heart. Hold the appliqué with tweezers, and apply dabs of glue to the wrong side .

design tip

A bucket bag has tall sides, a structured bottom, and an open top. Unfortunately, the sides of the bag are slouchy, even when laid on a flat surface. To aid in the stable placement of the appliqués, add structure to the bag. Insert either a cardboard box, enough tissue or giftwrap, or a small shopping bag to create support and provide a flat design surface.

3 Reposition the rose appliqué on the bag, and press it, glue side down, to adhere. Continue to position and adhere the remaining roses in the same manner, arranging them as shown in the layout diagram, or as desired.

4 Center the heart appliqué on the cuff of the bag. Position one 3-in.-wide scrollwork appliqué at each side of the heart. Use the iron to adhere the appliqués as in step 1.

An alternative approach to decorating a bucket bag is to apply an accent fabric to the cuff. The bag on these pages is made in a plain orange wool, so choosing a coordinating fabric is easy. Here, a leopard-print faux fur is adhered to the cuff using fabric glue and some machine stitching for reinforcement. Also consider using a wool in a bright color, a printed velvet, or a pinwale courdoroy.

Midnight Feather Clutch

Originally my mother's black gabardine clutch from the 1960s, this evening bag is restored to new elegance with layers and layers of lustrous black feathers. The feathers come attached to lightweight cardboard in an arc shape. When the feathered cards are layered, they create a romantic cascade of decoration. Rhinestone earrings in the Deco style (with posts removed) replace a broken clasp and add sparkle.

MATERIALS
- *12 cardboard arcs of hackle feathers in black, 2½" across*
- *6 sequin scallop shell appliqués in black, 2" high x 2" wide*
- *2 flat rhinestone earrings, ⅞" high x ⅝" wide*
- *Permanent adhesive*
- *Epoxy glue, 5-minute drying*

TOOLS
- *Tweezers*
- *Wire cutters*
- *Gloves*

THE FEATURED BAG
A softly structured clutch with a snap closure, approximately 6" high x 8" wide x 2" deep

decorating the midnight feather clutch

1 Place the bag right side up on a clean work surface. Turn one arc of feathers to the wrong side as shown, and apply permanent adhesive to the cardboard area that holds the feathers.

2 Turn the arc to the right side, and position it in the center of the bag so that the tips of the feathers are even with the bottom of the bag. Press the arc to adhere it to the bag.

4 Apply permanent adhesive to the wrong side of one sequin scallop shell. Position and adhere it to the right side of the clasp. Adhere a second shell to the left of the clasp and the third in the middle, as shown.

5 Use wire cutters to remove the post from one earring.

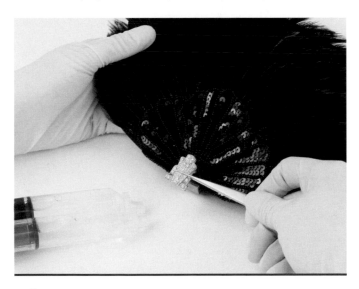

3 Working toward the clasp, continue to add five more arcs of feathers, overlapping them slightly. The sixth and final arc should butt up against the clasp at the top of the purse.

6 Put on protective gloves. Following the manufacturer's directions, hold the earring with the tweezers and apply epoxy to the back of the earring. Press the earring to the clasp to secure it in place. Repeat steps 1–6 to complete the other side of the bag.

variation

To add Old World glamour and elegance to a simple black evening bag, add a decorative hatpin. Found in a millinery store, this hatpin is made up of a black velvet flower accented with black sequins and "eyelash" and tail feathers. These over-dyed black feathers are particularly chic because the original iridescence of the natural feathers shines though.

Beaded Ballerina Bag

Reminiscent of the dramatic artistry of handmade ballet costumes, this unique little bag has couture style. It began as a humble drawstring pouch made from sheer peach fabric in a floral print. Each "flower" is outlined in silver bugle beads. Gray pearls and sparkling seed beads in plum and gold adorn the entire bag. Organdy ribbon in the sheerest cream color, narrow satin ribbon in salmon, and torn fabric strips in peach add casual chic.

MATERIALS
- 1 pkg. or 1,000 pale crystal iridescent cupped sequins, 5mm
- 1 hank of straight bugle beads in silver
- 3 4" vials of seed beads in assorted colors, size 11:
    plum
    pale blue
    gold
- 50 pearls in gray, 5mm dia.
- 10 glass beads with occlusions in peach, amber, and moss, 12 mm
- ¼ yd. polyester lining fabric to match bag
- 1 yd. of satin ribbon in peach, ⅛" wide
- 1 yard of organdy ribbon in cream, ¼" wide
- Thread in peach

TOOLS
- Scissors
- Beading needle

THE FEATURED BAG
A soft pouch with a pull-string closure, approximately 7" dia.

91

decorating the beaded ballerina bag

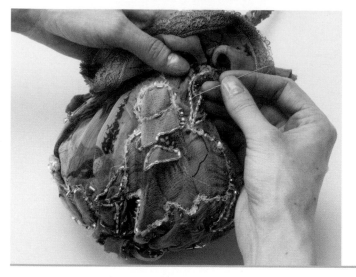

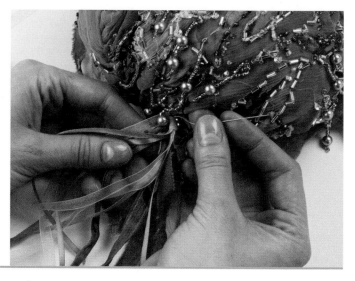

1 Use a threaded beading needle to randomly sew the sequins and bugle beads to the blue areas. Randomly sew the seed beads in plum, blue, and gold to areas of the bag, as desired.

2 Use a threaded beading needle to string four gold seed beads, one gray pearl, and 14 gold seed beads. Insert the needle into the fabric, and secure to make a dangling tassel. Repeat, as desired.

3 Tear eight strips of fabric, $1/2$ in. wide. Sew four strips to each side of the bag. Trim the length as desired. Sew a large glass bead to the end of each strip, sewing seed and bugle beads in a random pattern along the strip.

4 Sew several random lengths of satin and organdy ribbon to the bottom of the bag. Trim the ribbons and the strips of fabric to unequal lengths, with the longest streamer measuring 12 in., using scissors.

design tip

To tear fabric

more easily, measure and make tick marks

at even intervals along the cut edge of the fabric. Use scissors

to make 1-in.-long cuts at each mark to help start the tear for each strip.

Hold the fabric on both sides of the cut, and pull the fabric apart.

Tear along the straight of the goods

to ensure even strips.

variation

Tulle is a great way to add a hint of color and a fanciful touch to a fabric bag like this one. Inexpensive and readily available, tulle comes in a wide variety of colors that can enhance or slightly change the existing color of the bag. Experiment using different shades of tulle to see what looks best. Sew the tulle onto the bag, and decorate it with a sprinkling of beads.

Silver Moon Satin Clutch

This elegant clutch evokes the luxury and glamour of the 1930s when stars on the silver screen wore flowing satin gowns. Here, silver bugle beads trace the quilted pattern on lustrous satin fabric in the palest blue. Beaded "flowers" in quartz and silver seed beads add extra sparkle. A simple clasp made from clear Lucite embraced in silver bands completes the look. Florettes and silver seed beads adorn the bag frame.

MATERIALS
- 1 hank bugle beads in silver, size 2 (2mm x 4.5mm)
- 1 pkg. florette spacers in silver, 5mm
- 1 pkg. seed beads in silver, 2mm
- 9 beaded "flowers" in quartz and silver beads, ready-made or as desired
- 1 beaded "flower" in quartz with the stem and petals removed
- Thread in pale blue
- Permanent adhesive

TOOLS
- Scissors
- Beading needle
- Tweezers
- Optional: handmade beaded "flowers" (See page 134.)

THE FEATURED BAG
A quilted and lined satin bag with a snap closure, approximately 4" high x 8" wide at the top, 12" wide at the bottom

decorating the silver moon satin clutch

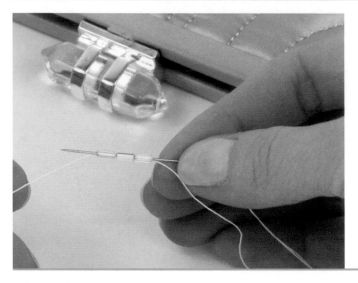

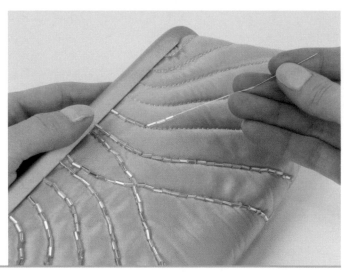

1 Using a beading needle and thread, take a few tiny stitches at the quilted stitches at the top edge of the bag. Slide three bugle beads onto the needle.

2 Slide the beads down to the quilted stitches on the bag, and sew a tiny stitch. Reload the needle with three more beads, and stitch to secure. Repeat to bead each quilted line on the bag.

5 Apply a dab of glue to the wrong side of the stemless bead-ed flower. Use the tweezers to position and press the flower below the clasp.

design tip

To prevent the bugle beads from buckling or creating an uneven line on the fabric, leave a tiny space between the three-bead sections as you sew. This space will provide just enough ease so that the beads lay flat.

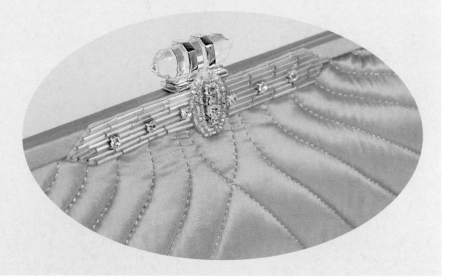

3 Add a scant dab of glue to the wrong side of one beaded "flower." Glue it to the bag. Secure it with hand stitches. Add the remaining beaded flowers in the same way.

4 Position and glue the florettes to the frame of the bag at even intervals, adding a small silver bead to the center of each florette using tweezers and glue.

variation

To enjoy the elaborate look of beads without having to sew or glue on each bead one at a time, consider using a beaded appliqué decoration. Here, a narrow appliqué in monochromatic silver fits perfectly along the frame below the clasp. Rows of long silver bugle beads are combined with large and small rhinestones. The entire appliqué is quickly affixed with permanent adhesive.

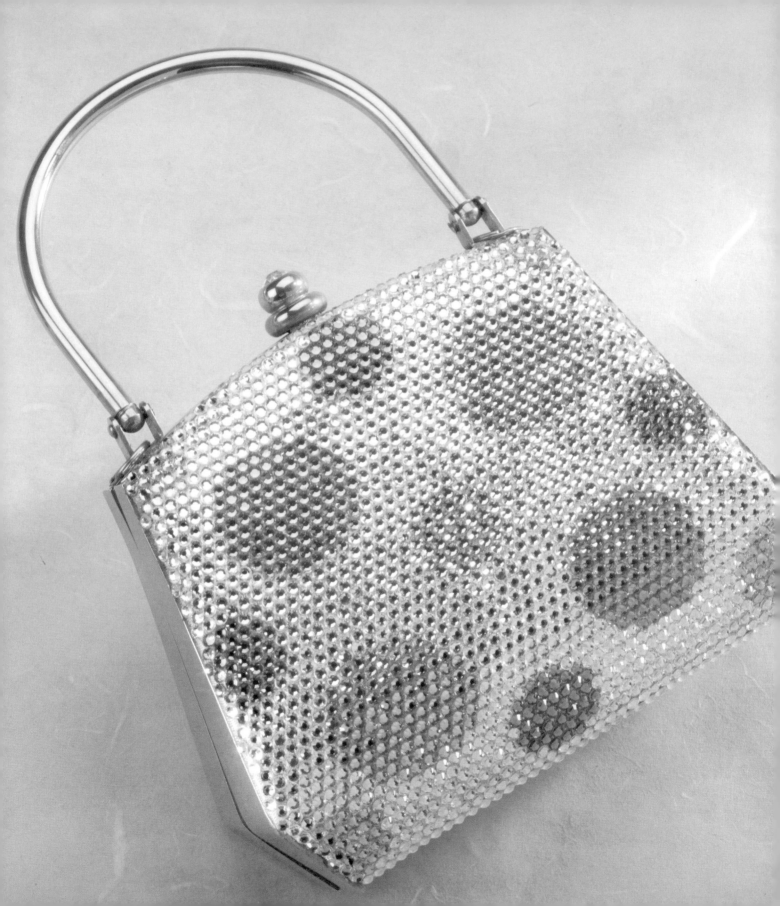

Pavé Polka-Dot Purse

This dazzling showpiece, paved in crystal rhinestones, boasts a whimsical polka-dot pattern in rosy pink, light sapphire blue, bright apple green, and deep purple surrounded by a sea of sparkling silver. This purse began as a classic, tailored evening bag in a metallic fabric with a silver frame and a stunning rhinestone clasp. When rhinestones are applied to the front and back of the bag, it is easy to mistake it for an haute couture look-alike.

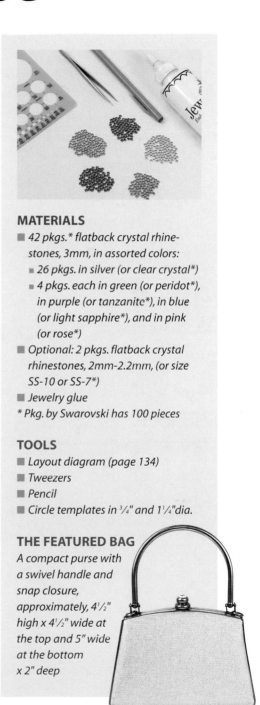

MATERIALS
- 42 pkgs.* flatback crystal rhinestones, 3mm, in assorted colors:
  - 26 pkgs. in silver (or clear crystal*)
  - 4 pkgs. each in green (or peridot*), in purple (or tanzanite*), in blue (or light sapphire*), and in pink (or rose*)
- Optional: 2 pkgs. flatback crystal rhinestones, 2mm-2.2mm, (or size SS-10 or SS-7*)
- Jewelry glue
* Pkg. by Swarovski has 100 pieces

TOOLS
- Layout diagram (page 134)
- Tweezers
- Pencil
- Circle templates in ¾" and 1¼"dia.

THE FEATURED BAG
A compact purse with a swivel handle and snap closure, approximately, 4½" high x 4½" wide at the top and 5" wide at the bottom x 2" deep

decorating the pavé polka dot purse

advisory

Before beginning this project

The rhinestones are laid out in rows in a sweep across the surface of the bag to create a honeycomb pattern. Make certain that each new rhinestone you place touches a previously placed rhinestone with no spaces or gaps in between. When starting a new row, neatly fit the rhinestones in the spaces provided by the row above. Do not skip from one side of the bag to the other. Do not fill in either the polka-dots or the background first. This will cause the pattern to be misaligned.

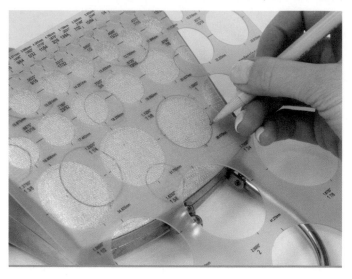

1 Following the layout diagram on page 134, use a pencil and the template to trace the large and small circles on one side of the bag.

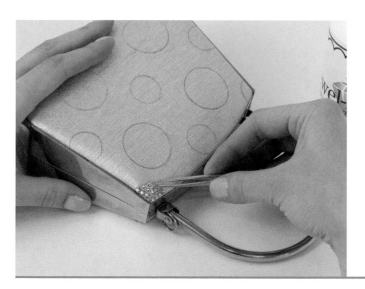

3 Using tweezers, pick up a green rhinestone and apply a dab of adhesive to the wrong side. Beginning at the top corner of the bag, position and press the rhinestone, glue side down, to the marked polka-dot. Continue to glue on green rhinestones.

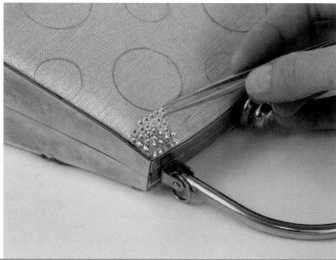

4 Apply the silver rhinestones in the same manner. Upon reaching the edge of the next polka-dot, follow the layout diagram to fill it in with the appropriate color rhinestone.

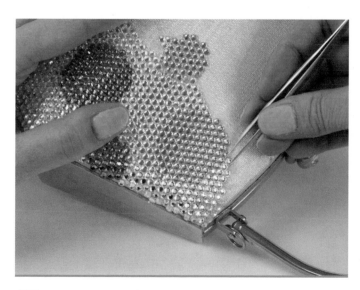

2 Repeat step 1 to trace both the large and small circles on the other side of the bag.

5 Continue applying rhinestones following the layout diagram until the entire side of the bag is paved in rhinestones. To fill in any bare areas near the edge of the bag, use the optional rhinestones. Repeat steps 1–5 to do the other side of the bag.

variation

Structured handbags covered in fabric can be covered in any kind of bead or rhinestone. Simply glue them in place using a permanent jewelry adhesive. To create a monochromatic look like the one featured here, intermix jewelry findings and sparkling rhinestones. Findings have interesting textural details and finishes, adding luster; rhinestones throw off glints of light.

Marabou Minibag

Glamorous and elegant yet funky and fun, this feather boa bag makes an ideal evening bag as well as a great accessory for everday wear. Originally a simple black pull-string bag, the Marabou Minibag is created by concealing the foundation felt with a boa of marabou feathers. The boa is coiled around the bag and stitched to the outside fabric. A handle made up of strands of seed beads in lush purple adds extra sparkle.

MATERIALS
- Marabou boa in plum, 2 yds. long
- 1 yd. satin ribbon in black, 2" wide
- 1 hank seed beads in plum, size 11
- 1 spool nylon bead cord, size 0
- Thread in black

TOOLS
- Scissors
- Hand sewing needle
- Beading needle
- Sewing machine

THE FEATURED BAG
A soft pouch in black felt with ribbon pull-strings, approximately
5" high x 5" wide

decorating the marabou minibag

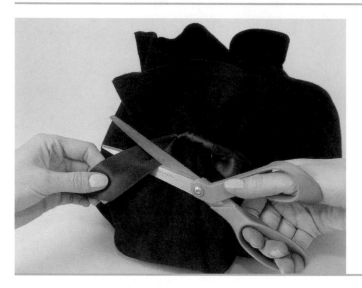

1 Adjust the size of the bag opening by pulling on the pair of ribbons at each side of the casing. Secure the opening by tying the ribbons into knots, cutting off all but 2 in.

2 Beginning at the top edge, lay one end of the boa against the bag and use a threaded needle to tack it securely in place using a whip stitch.

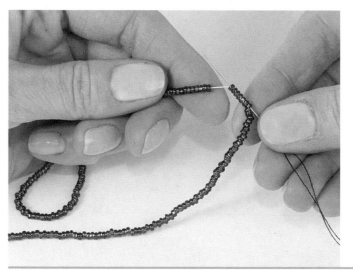

4 Use a beading needle double-threaded with nylon cord to restring each strand of seed beads, leaving a 6-in. tail on each strand and knotting each end. Gather the knotted ends of the strands together, and fold them in half. Tie the ends together.

5 To make the handle, position the fold of the beaded strands on the inside of the bag. Use a threaded needle to lash the strands in place, using an overhand stitch. Repeat to secure the knotted ends of the strands to the opposite side of the bag.

3 Coil 4 in. of the boa around the bag, and use an overhand stitch to sew the section in place. Continue to coil and sew the boa to the bag until the bag is concealed. Snip off the extra boa.

6 To reinforce the handle, cut two 2-in. lengths of ribbon; set one aside. Position one length over the ends of the strands on the inside of the bag, and machine-stitch as shown. Repeat to secure the strands to the opposite side of the bag.

variation

A handle can change the look of a bag entirely. Instead of attaching a handle made of beaded strands, use extra-wide silk ribbon instead. For a different look, use strands of pearls or a silver chainlink bracelet. Match the scale and size of the bag to the handle, coordinating dainty handles with delicate bags, and heavy handles with larger bags.

design tip

A flexible boa of feathers can be sewn to any soft, round handbag. If the bag is made of a hard material, use permanent adhesive to secure the boa to the surface of the bag.

Tottenham Tweed Clutch

A smart-looking handbag is transformed simply and elegantly using a vintage costume jewelry necklace. The centerpiece of the decoration is a "grape cluster" made up of a combination of bronze, metallic, blue, and faceted crystal beads accented by dainty leaves in iridescent teal and silver. The restrained color of the beaded detail adds a lustrous counterpoint to the classic tweed fabric in blue and black.

MATERIALS
- Beaded costume jewelry necklace with grape cluster, or 24 beads in blue and bronze tones, 1cm–6mm dia.
- Permanent adhesive
- Thread in a coordinating color

TOOLS
- Scissors
- Pencil
- Bent-nose chain pliers
- Hand sewing needle

THE FEATURED BAG
A tweed-covered structured clutch with a snap closure, approximately 4$\frac{1}{2}$" high x 10" wide x 2$\frac{1}{2}$" deep

decorating the tottenham tweed clutch

1 Center the brooch part of the necklace on the front edge of the bag, allowing the beaded strands to rest at each side. Use a pencil to mark the end bead at each side.

2 Carefully remove the sections of the clasp, using scissors to cut the strands. Hold the marked bead, and slide the excess beads off the necklace at each side.

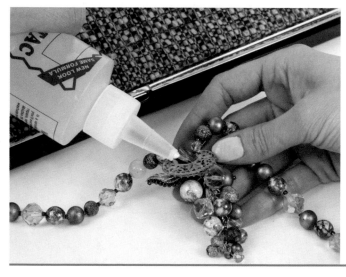

4 Apply a light coat of adhesive to the wrong side of the "grape cluster" brooch. Position and press the cluster, glue side down, to the center front edge of the bag.

5 Apply a small dab of glue to the wrong side of each bead, one at a time, and press them to the bag. Let the glue dry.

3 Tie a knot in the cord at each end to secure the beads. Add a scant dab of glue to the knotted ends. Let the glue dry.

6 For extra security, use a threaded needle to tack the beaded strands to the fabric.

To better secure the beaded strand in step 3, bring the cord around and through the final bead before tying the knot. The wrap will trap the last bead.

design tip

*To better secure the
beaded strand in step 3, bring
the cord around and through the final
bead before tying the knot. The wrap
will trap the last bead.*

variation

Another appealing embellishment for a bag with a patterned or busy fabric is a leather "flower." Featured here in rich teal blue, the lush leather petals are layered and form a sumptuous rose. Purchased at a millinery supply store and intended for a hat, the flower lends a touch of romance to the bag. To add a rose to your bag, apply adhesive to the wrong side of your flower and press it to the bag, glue side down, in a desired position.

Mini Travel Valise

A traveling exhibition of luggage tags, stamps, and vintage ephemera from around the world showcases the exotic destinations one often dreams of visiting. Here, images are affixed to a little papier-mâché box that has been painted to resemble a worn leather steamer trunk. The result is a handbag that looks as though it has crisscrossed the globe. Leather handles and a decorative clasp add more charm to this sturdy little bag.

MATERIALS
- Acrylic paint, 2-oz. bottles: in brown, caramel, cream, and white
- 4 grommets in brass, $\frac{1}{2}$" dia. with a $\frac{3}{8}$" opening
- 1 flat wooden hoop, 1" dia.
- Brown twine
- Printed images with a travel theme
- Decoupage glue
- 1 brown leather handle, 7" long
- 2 bolts with nuts, $\frac{5}{8}$" long with decorative heads (for latch)
- 2 brass bolts with nuts, $\frac{5}{8}$" long with $\frac{1}{2}$" head (for handle)

TOOLS
- Layout diagram (page 135)
- 2 brushes: paint; sponge ■ Ruler
- Decoupage scissors ■ Hammer
- Block of wood ■ Grommet tool for $\frac{3}{8}$" grommets ■ Permanent adhesive
- Decoupage scissors ■ Tweezers

THE FEATURED BAG
A papier-mâché box with in a trunk style, approximately 5" high x 8" wide x 5" deep

decorating the mini travel valise

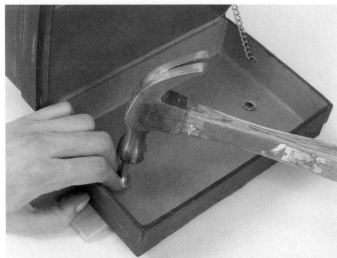

1 Apply two coats of brown paint to the outside of the box, allowing the paint to dry between coats. Simulate wear at the edges of the box by applying smudges of light-colored paint.

2 In the box, use the points of scissors to pierce two very small holes, 1 in. from each short side. Install a grommet in each hole, following the manufacturer instructions.

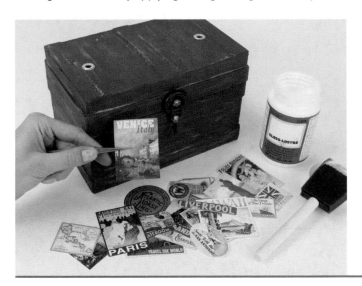

4 Cut out approximately 40 travel images using scissors. Apply decoupage glue to the wrong side of one image and apply it to the box with tweezers. Smooth the image to adhere. See the layout diagram on page 135 for a guide to placing the images.

5 Apply a thin, even coat of glue to the entire surface area of the box using the foam brush. Let the glue dry completely. Apply a second coat, and let it dry completely. Repeat to seal the interior surfaces of the box.

3 Install two grommets on the box and lid. Insert a bolt through each grommet and fasten with a nut, allowing ⅛-in. play. Glue on the hoop, and add a loop of twine for a closure.

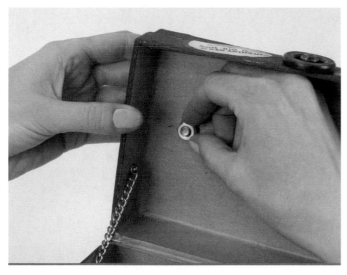

6 Set the closed box on a flat surface. Secure each end of the handle to the lid by inserting a bolt through each handle end loop and the grommet hole. Secure each bolt at the inside using a nut. Reattach the twine loop to the front of the bag.

variation

For a decidedly different take, try a floral theme. Here, a wooden box is painted mint-green and allowed to dry. Precut rose motifs are applied in a pleasing arrangement using decoupage glue. A sealer coat of the same glue protects the images. A beaded handle with a ribbon bow is attached to the lid.

design tip

Do not attempt to cut any image coated with wet glue; it will tear. Instead, let the glue dry completely. Then use a sharp blade or decoupage scissors to cut the image as desired.

Making Designer Bags

Bejeweled Evening Bag

See page 12

You will love making this bag, and you will especially enjoy working with silk velvet, which is so soft to the touch. Velvet has a nap that will shimmer with color and light. It is important to handle velvet with some care to avoid marring its surface. Use straight pins intended for silk fabric; they will not leave holes. Also, never place an iron directly on velvet.

MATERIALS

- ¼ yd. silk velvet in green
- ¼ yd. faux leopard print
- Thread in green
- Purse frame in gold

TOOLS

- Pattern (See page 128.)
- Straight pins for silk
- Scissors
- Sewing machine
- Hand sewing needle
- Flat-head screwdriver

THE FEATURED BAG

6½" high x 7" wide x 4" deep

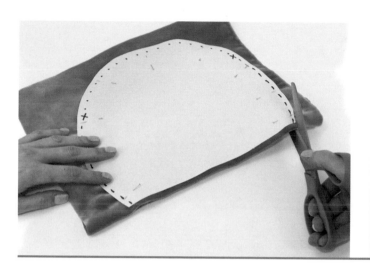

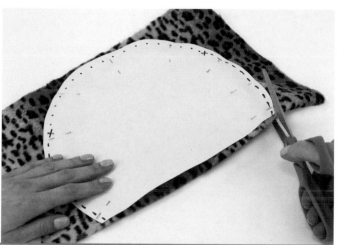

1 Fold the velvet in half, wrong sides together, all edges even. Lay the pattern on the fold as indicated; secure it with straight pins. Cut along the solid line through both layers of fabric.

2 Repeat step 1 using the pattern to cut out the bag lining from the leopard print velvet, cutting along the fold line to make two lining pieces.

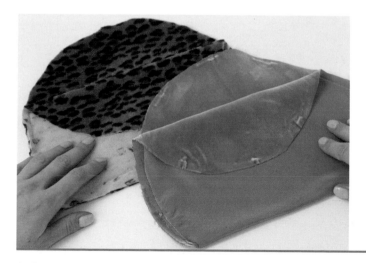

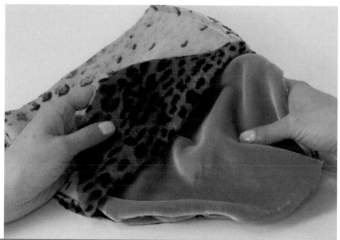

3 Fold the bag piece in half along the fold, right sides together. Pin, then machine-stitch from the fold to the marked "X" on each side, 1/4 in. from the edge. Repeat for the bag lining.

4 Turn the bag right side out. Slip it inside the lining, right sides together, and align the open curved edges.

making the bejeweled evening bag

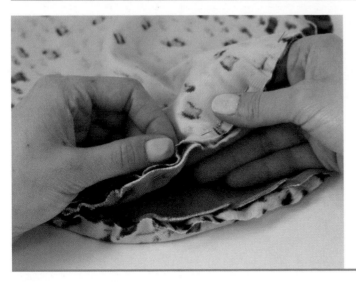

5 Pin the bag and the lining together along the curved edges.

6 Machine stitch ¹/₄ in. from the curved edges all around. Remove the pins as you sew.

9 Use a needle with a doubled and knotted thread to sew a running stitch along the bottom of the bag at the fold line. Pull the thread to form soft folds. Take a few stitches to secure the gather.

10 Use a needle with a doubled and knotted thread to sew a running stitch along the mouth of the bag. Pull the thread to gather the edge. Do not cut the thread.

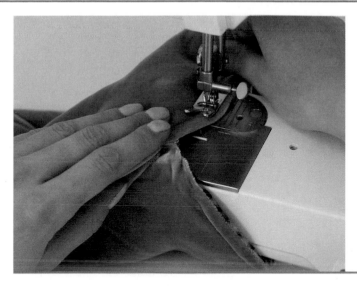

7 Turn the bag lining to the right side, and tuck it inside the bag. Smooth the fabrics flat. Top-stitch around the mouth of the bag, $1/8$ in. from the edge.

8 Sew on the brooch and the earrings (and any other decoration desired) to the bag only; keep the lining free so that no stitches show on the inside of the bag.

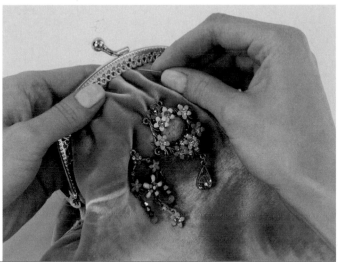

11 Push the lining back into the bag. Center the purse over the curved edges that form the mouth of the bag. Push each curved edge into the channel of the frame, easing the gather as needed, using the flat head of the screwdriver. Cut the thread.

12 Hand-sew the frame to the bag with matching thread. Poke the needle through the holes in the frame to catch the bag and lining fabrics securely. To finish, use a double threaded needle to sew beads to the bottom gather, as desired.

Blue Suede Portfolio

See page 40

The ease of working with faux suede is immediately evident when you cut the fabric using a rotary cutter. Faux suede does not ravel or fray, its edge remains clean and neat after cutting. The layers of fabric here are laminated to provide a sturdy, triple layer of fabric with extra structure to form the folio-style bag.

MATERIALS
- Faux suede:
  - 1/2 yd. blue faux suede
  - 1/2 yd. yellow faux suede
  - 1/2 yd. blackout curtain lining
- Spray Adhesive
- Thread in blue

TOOLS
- Pattern (See page 129.)
- Straight pins
- Rotary cutter
- Self-healing mat
- Ruler
- Scissors
- Sewing machine

THE FEATURED BAG
11" high x 13" wide

making the blue suede portfolio

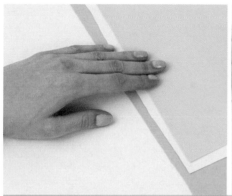  

1 Cut three rectangles, each 34 in. by 13 in., from the blue suede, the yellow suede, and the curtain lining fabric. Lay the yellow suede, wrong side up, on a work surface. Lay the curtain lining on a second protected surface, and apply a coat of adhesive. Press the lining, tacky side down, on the yellow suede; smooth to adhere it. Adhere the opposite side of the lining to the blue suede in the same way (above left). Position the pattern on the laminated fabrics. Cut around the pattern using a rotary cutter (above right). Set the fabrics aside.

2 Use a rotary cutter to cut out a $1/4$-in.-wide-by-13-in.-long strip from the fabrics. Adhere it as shown on page 40.

3 Sew a decorative line of stitching $1/4$ in. from the edge of the portfolio piece all around.

4 Lay the portfolio piece on a flat surface, yellow side up. Fold up the bottom third and secure the sides with pins. Overstitch the machine stitching on the two short sides, stopping at the Xs marked on the pattern.

5 Fold over the top third of the bag to close the folio.

Urban Cowgirl Saddle Bag

See page 64

*This saddle bag is fun and easy to make,
especially in a faux suede fabric in a luscious tangerine orange.
The main bag is made in two sections, and the rows of fringe are
added before the bag is stitched together.*

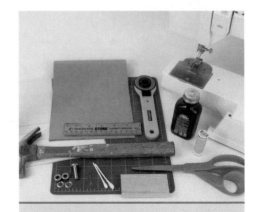

MATERIALS
- 1 yd. faux suede in orange
- Thread in orange
- 2 grommets in brass, ³⁄₈" inner dia.
- Contact cement

TOOLS
- Patterns (See page 130.)
- Straight pins
- Rotary cutter
- Self-healing mat
- Rotary cutting ruler
- Pencil
- Cotton swabs
- Scissors
- Sewing machine
- Seam ripper
- Sewing machine
- Grommet kit or block of wood, grommet tool for ³⁄₈" grommets, and hammer
- Tape

THE FEATURED BAG
11¹⁄₂" high x 10" wide

making the urban cowgirl saddle bag

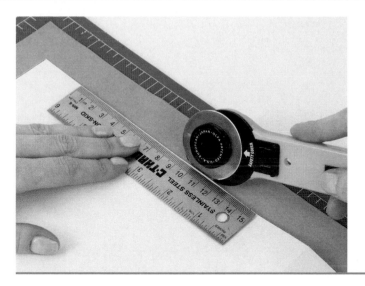

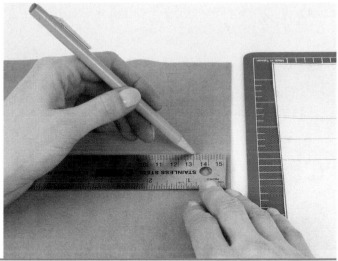

1 Place the faux suede on the self-healing mat. Position the bag front and bag back patterns on top. Secure them with pins. Use a rotary cutter and straight edge to cut out both pieces.

2 Lay the bag front piece right side up on a flat work surface. Use a ruler and pencil to mark four fringe lines on the suede, as indicated on the pattern. Repeat for the bag back piece.

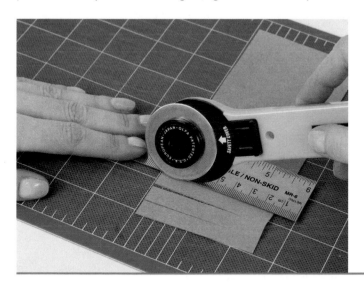

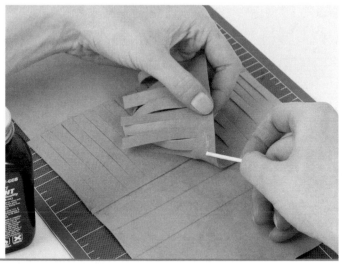

3 Use a rotary cutter, a straight edge, and a cutting mat to cut eight 10-in.-by-4 1/2-in. rectangles from the remaining suede. Follow the pattern to make 1/4-in.-wide cuts, stopping 1/2 in. from the edge. Repeat with the remaining rectangles.

4 Apply a thin line of cement across the top edge of one fringe piece. Place the fringe on the bag front, glue side down, even with the lowest fringe line. Adhere three more fringe sections to the bag front. Repeat for the back. Let the glue dry.

making the urban cowgirl saddle bag

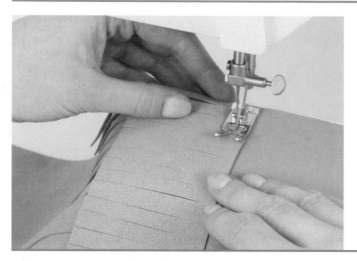

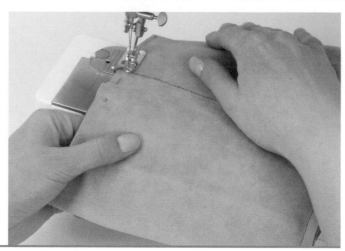

5 Top-stitch each section of fringe to the bag along the top edge of the fringe, ³/₈ in. from the edge, using a sewing machine. Repeat for the front of the bag.

6 Lay the bag, right side up, on a work surface. Lay the bag front on top, right sides together and with the fringe and edges aligned. Secure them with pins. Machine-stitch the side and bottom edges with a ³/₈-in. seam allowance to create the pouch of the bag. Turn the bag to the right side.

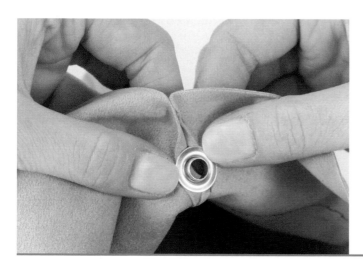

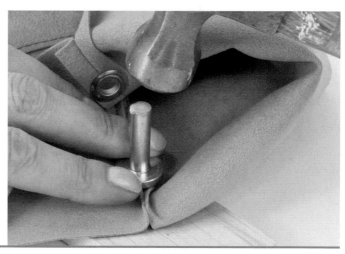

9 Flatten the seam around the grommet on the inside of the bag, and lay the ring part of the grommet on the neck.

10 Place the wooden block on the work surface, and position the grommet on the block. Follow the manufacturer's directions to secure the grommet in place. Repeat to secure the second grommet to the opposite side of the bag.

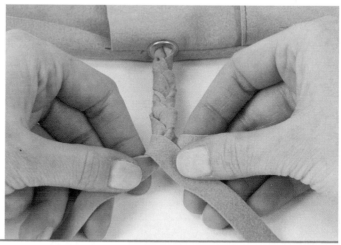

7 Use the seam ripper to open each side seam just enough to insert the grommet, 1¹/₄ in. from the top edge. Err on the side of making the openings too small.

8 Insert the neck of a grommet into the opening in the seam.

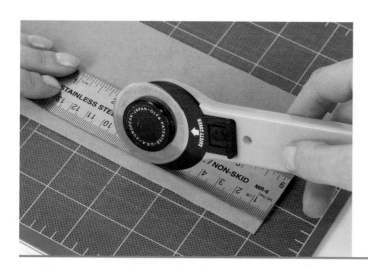

11 Use the rotary cutter and the straight edge to cut nine 14-in.-by-¹/₄-in. strips from suede. Gather three strips, and make a knot 1 in. from one end. Thread the ends into the grommet at the inside of the bag, exiting to the outside.

12 Braid the strips, and secure them with tape. Repeat at the opposite grommet. Add more braided sections to make a long strap as shown on page 64, removing the tape and knotting the ends together.

Springtime Pull-String Bag

See page 70

*The pull-string bag is an
amazingly versatile bag in that
it is easy to make in practically any size.
The bag opens and closes smoothly by pulling on the strings
or ribbons threaded through the casing at the top.
Consider sheer fabrics for your bags. Or choose velvets and silks,
adding beads and other trim. Make one or several for keeping
cosmetics, mementos, and jewelry.*

MATERIALS
- Cotton fabric:
  ½ yd. with polka-dot pattern
  ½ yd. in white for lining
- Thread in white
- 1½ yds. grosgrain ribbon in green,
  ⅝" wide

TOOLS
- Pattern for bag (See page131.)
- Pattern for casing (see page131.)
- Scissors
- Straight pins
- Sewing machine
- Household iron
- Hand sewing needle
- 2 safety pins

THE FEATURED BAG
8½" high x 9" wide

making the springtime pull-string bag

 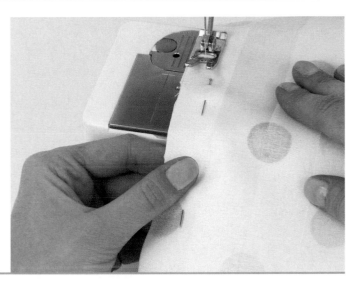

1 Place the pattern on the polka-dot fabric. Secure it with pins. Cut out the bag piece. Repeat to cut out the bag lining from the white lining fabric.

2 Place the bag and the lining pieces, right sides together, with edges even. Secure them with pins. Machine-stitch $1/4$ in. from the edge on all sides, leaving a 2-in. opening for turning.

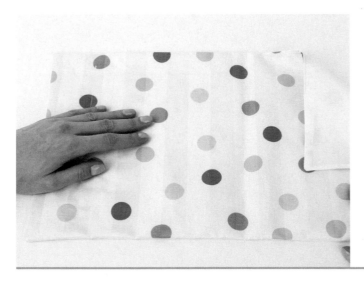 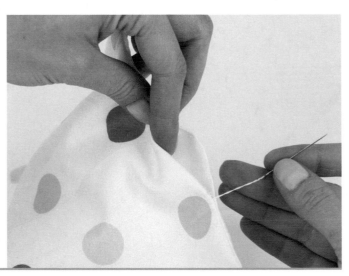

3 Turn the sewn sections to the right side through the opening.

4 Use a needle and thread to sew the opening closed.

making the springtime pull-string bag

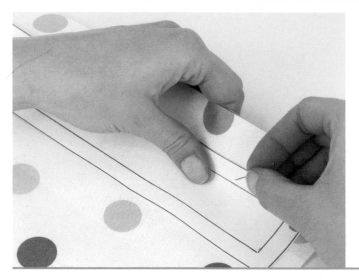

5 Fold the remaining polka-dot fabric in half. Place the casing pattern on top, and secure it with pins. Cut through both layers to make two casing pieces.

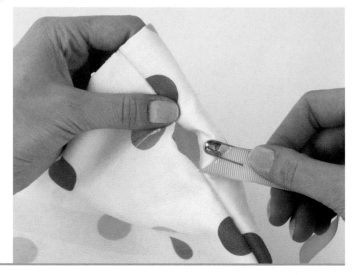

6 Place one casing section on a flat surface, wrong side up. Fold each raw edge $1/2$ in. to the wrong side. Press with an iron. Repeat for the second casing section.

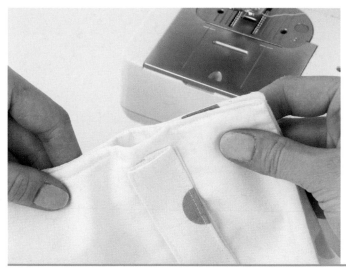

9 Fold the bag in half, right sides together and edges even. Machine-stitch the short side edges with a $1/4$-in. seam allowance; leave 1-in. opening on each side where the casings are joined. Turn the bag to the right side.

10 Measure and cut two 24-in. lengths of ribbon. Attach a safety pin to the end of one ribbon.

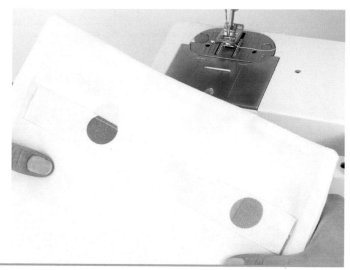

7 Lay the bag section, lining up, on a flat surface. Place and pin a casing piece parallel with and 2 in. below the top short edge. Repeat for the second casing at the opposite short side.

8 Machine-stitch the casings ⅛ in. from each long folded edge.

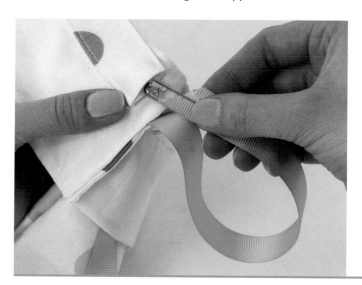

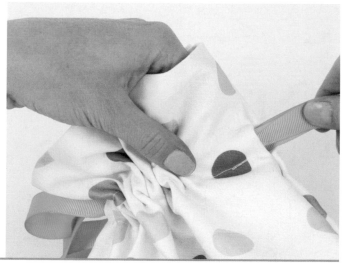

11 Insert the safety pin into the casing at the inside of the bag, and work it through its entire length.

12 Exit the casing, and pull the ribbon until there are equal lengths of ribbon at each side of the bag. Repeat steps 11 and 12 at the second casing. Pull on the ribbons to gather the bag, tying bows at each side to close.

Patterns and Diagrams

Bejeweled Evening Bag

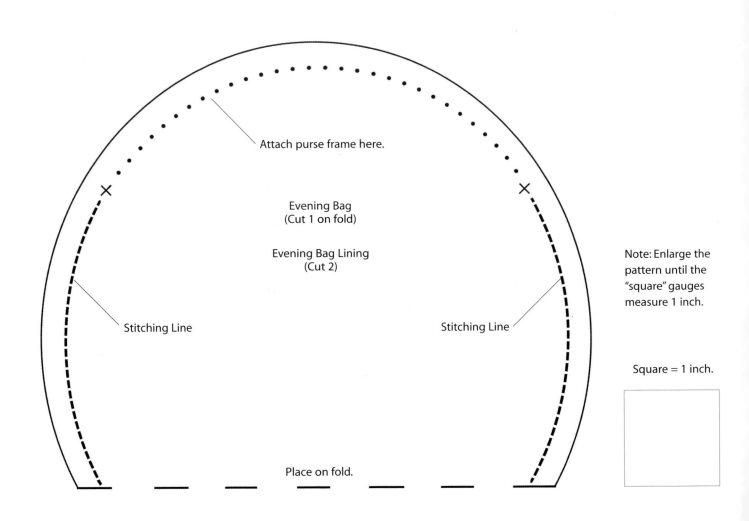

Attach purse frame here.

Evening Bag
(Cut 1 on fold)

Evening Bag Lining
(Cut 2)

Stitching Line

Stitching Line

Note: Enlarge the pattern until the "square" gauges measure 1 inch.

Square = 1 inch.

Place on fold.

Blue Suede Portfolio

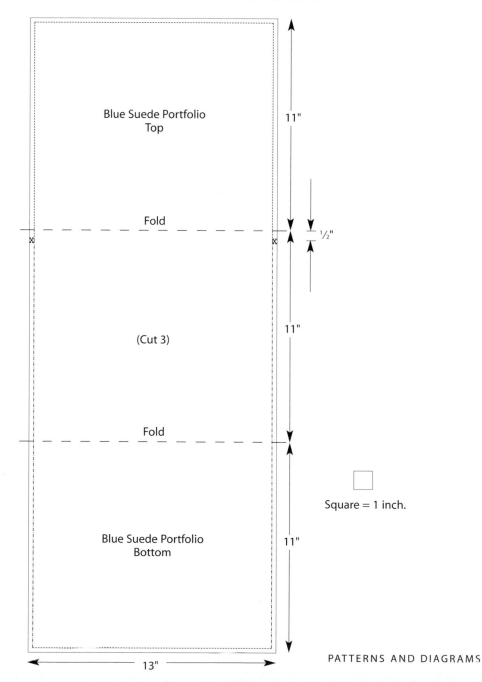

Blue Suede Portfolio
Top

11"

Fold

½"

(Cut 3)

11"

Fold

Square = 1 inch.

Blue Suede Portfolio
Bottom

11"

13"

Urban Cowgirl Saddle Bag

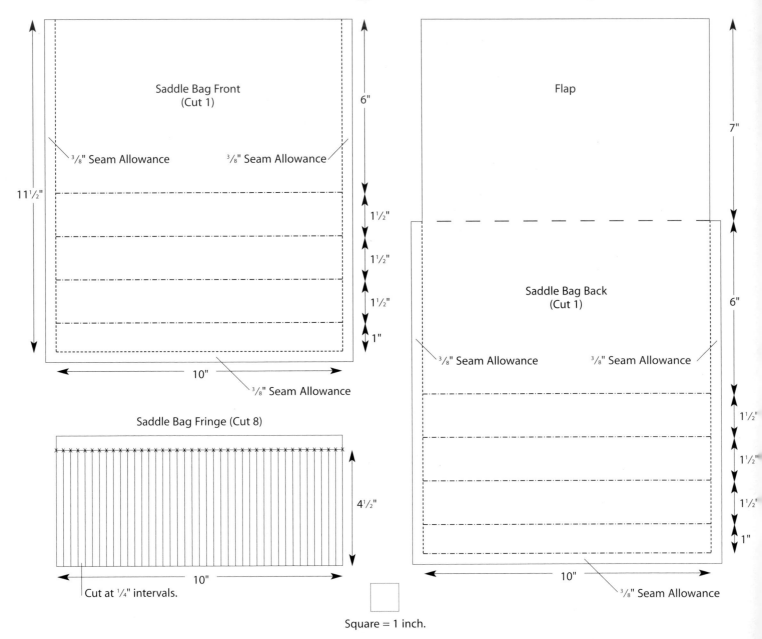

Saddle Bag Front
(Cut 1)

³⁄₈" Seam Allowance   ³⁄₈" Seam Allowance

6"

1¹⁄₂"

1¹⁄₂"

1¹⁄₂"

1"

11¹⁄₂"

10"

³⁄₈" Seam Allowance

Flap

7"

Saddle Bag Back
(Cut 1)

³⁄₈" Seam Allowance   ³⁄₈" Seam Allowance

6"

1¹⁄₂"

1¹⁄₂"

1¹⁄₂"

1"

10"

³⁄₈" Seam Allowance

Saddle Bag Fringe (Cut 8)

4¹⁄₂"

10"

Cut at ¹⁄₄" intervals.

Square = 1 inch.

Springtime Pull-String Bag

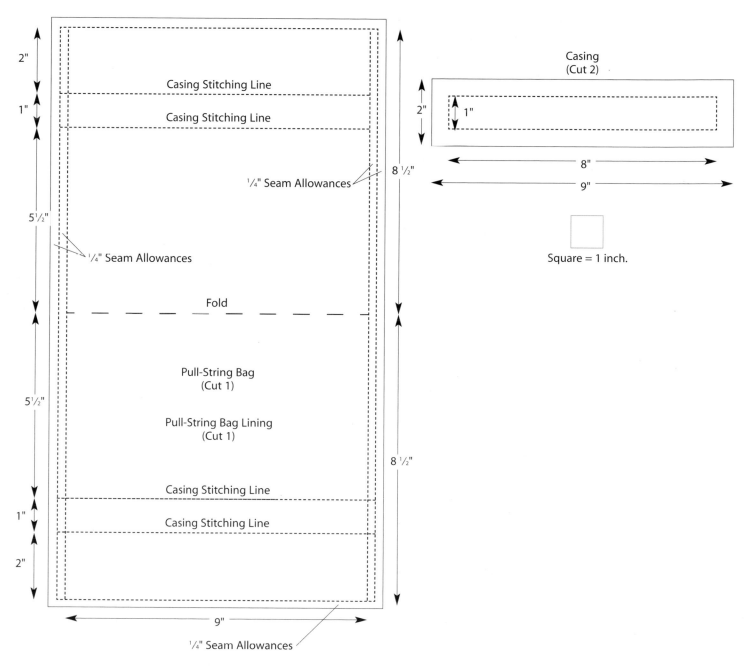

2"

1"

Casing Stitching Line

Casing Stitching Line

$1/4$" Seam Allowances

8 1/2"

5 1/2"

$1/4$" Seam Allowances

Fold

Pull-String Bag
(Cut 1)

Pull-String Bag Lining
(Cut 1)

5 1/2"

8 1/2"

Casing Stitching Line

Casing Stitching Line

1"

2"

9"

$1/4$" Seam Allowances

Casing
(Cut 2)

2"

1"

8"

9"

Square = 1 inch.

"Miss Kitty" Art

Blue-Boots
Tote Art

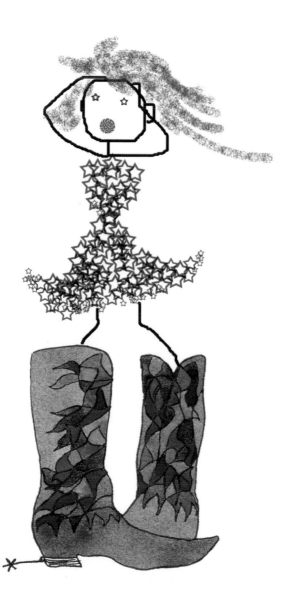

Folk Art Bucket Bag
Diagram

Satin Moon Clutch Beading Diagram

The principle of making any beaded flower is shown here using large beads so that the technique is clear. You can substitute different beads to make a beaded flower of your own design.

MATERIALS
- *7 large round beads*
- *Optional: small beads for "stem"*
- *Wire that passes through holes in beads*

TOOLS
- *Wire cutters*

1 Thread a bead on a 5-in. length of wire so that a 1¹/₂-in. tail extends beyond the hole. Bring the short tail around the bead, and twist it around the long wire.

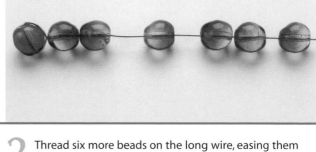

2 Thread six more beads on the long wire, easing them past the twisted part of the wire at the base of the bead strung in step 1.

3 Thread the end of the long wire back through the first bead as shown. Carefully pull the wire to form a circle of beads around the first bead.

4 Secure the circle of beads by threading the long wire between two beads, making one wind and allowing the long wire to extend from between the beads. Optional: add smaller beads to the stem of the "flower."

Pavé Polka-Dot Purse Diagram

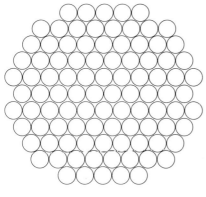

Row 1   5 rhinestones
Row 2   8 rhinestones
Row 3   9 rhinestones
Row 4   10 rhinestones
Row 5   11 rhinestones
Row 6   10 rhinestones
Row 7   11 rhinestones
Row 8   10 rhinestones
Row 9   9 rhinestones
Row 10 8 rhinestones
Row 11 5 rhinestones

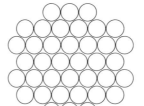

Row 1   3 rhinestones
Row 2   6 rhinestones
Row 3   7 rhinestones
Row 4   6 rhinestones
Row 5   7 rhinestones
Row 6   6 rhinestones
Row 7   3 rhinestones

Mini Travel Valise Diagram

FRONT

BACK

TOP

SIDE

SIDE

Bejeweled Evening Bag p. 12

Victorian Straw Tote p. 16

Big-City Bowling Bag p. 20

Hollywood Hatbox p. 24

"Miss Kitty" Tote p. 28

American Beauty Bag p. 32

Mod Print Tote p. 36

Blue Suede Portfolio p. 40

Tropical Demi p. 42

Blue-Boots Tote p. 46

Buttoned-Up Hobo Bag p. 50

Swingtime Shoulder Bag p. 56

Lush Leopard Hatbox p. 60

Urban Cowgirl Saddlebag p. 64

Girly Weekender p. 66

Springtime Pull-String Bag p. 70

Snow-Flurry Lipstick Purse p. 74

Vintage Rhinestone Purse p. 78

Folk Art Bucket Bag p. 82

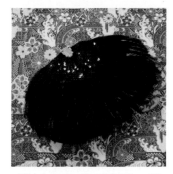

Midnight Feather Clutch p. 86

Beaded Ballerina Bag p. 90

Silver Moon Satin Clutch p. 94

Pavé Polka-Dot Purse p. 98

Marabou Minibag p. 102

An Illustrated Glossary of the Collection

Whether it's an elegant clutch for an evening out, or a roomy tote for a weekend out of town, there is sure to be a bag that inspires you in The Collection.

Tottenham Tweed Clutch p. 106

Mini Travel Valise p. 110

Beaded Gingham Bag
(Bejeweled Evening Bag p. 12)

Summer Day Straw Tote
(Victorian Straw Tote p. 16)

Pink Poodle Purse
(Big-City Bowling Bag p. 20)

Monogram Hatbox
(Hollywood Hatbox p. 24)

Crocheted Keychain Tote
("Miss Kitty" Tote p. 28)

Pastel Tassel Purse
(American Beauty Bag p. 32)

Cool Jewel Tote
(Mod Print Tote p. 36)

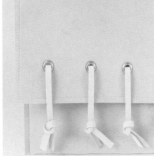
Sleek Suede Clutch
(Blue Suede Portfolio p. 40)

Sequin Rose Demi
(Tropical Demi p. 42)

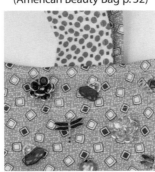
Charming Tote
(Blue-Boots Tote p. 46)

Pom-Pom Hobo Bag
(Buttoned-Up Hobo Bag p. 50)

Vintage Lace Shoulder Bag
(Swingtime Shoulder Bag p. 56)

Safari Hatbox
(Lush Leopard Hatbox p. 60)

Tin Star Saddle Bag
(Urban Cowgirl Saddle Bag p. 64)

Pink Tropics Tote
(Girly Weekender p. 66)

Velvet Blossom Pull-String Bag
(Springtime Pull String Bag p. 70)

Refined Rhinestone Lipstick Purse
(Snow-Flurry Lipstick Pursep. 74)

Elegant Heirloom Purse
(Vintage Rhinestone Purse p. 78)

Cozy Fur Cuff Bucket Bag
(Folk Art Bucket Bag p. 82)

Fabulous 40s Hatpin Clutch
(Midnight Feather Clutch p. 86)

Beaded Tulle Bag
(Ballerina Bag p. 90)

Art Deco Clutch
(Silver Moon Satin Clutch p. 94)

Shimmering Silver Purse
(Pavé Polka-Dot Purse p. 98)

Satin Handle Boa Bag
(Marabou Minibag p. 102)

Blue Rose Clutch
(Tottenham Tweed Clutch p. 106)

Romantic Rose Box Purse
(Mini Travel Valise p. 110)

An Illustrated Glossary of the Variations

Inspired by the bags in The Collection, these creative alternatives to the original designs will encourage your creativity. Use beads, rhinestones, trims, and appliqués to turn any bag into an expression of your own individual style.

Sources and Resources

Beacon Adhesives Company
P.O. Box 2500
Mt. Vernon, NY 10550
914-699-3400
www.beaconadhesives.com
Magna-Tac 809™ Permanent Adhesive
(Hollywood Hatbox, page 24;
Miss Kitty Tote, page 28;
Blue-Boots Tote, page 46;
Girly Weekender, page 66;
Folk Art Bucket Bag, page 82;
Midnight Feather Clutch, page 86;
Silver Moon Satin Clutch, page 94;
Tottenham Tweed Clutch, page 106)

B&J Fabrics
525 7th Ave., 2nd Floor
New York, NY 10019
212-354-8150
www.bandjfabrics.com
Velvet, gingham, "Chanel" suiting fabric,
wool felt, faux suede, polka-dot fabric,
faux fur, tulle
(Bejeweled Evening Bag, page 12;
Beaded Gingham Bag, page 15;
Big-City Bowling Bag, page 20;
Miss Kitty Tote, page 28;
Blue Suede Portfolio, page 40;
Sleek Suede Clutch, page 43;
Urban Cowgirl Saddle Bag, page 64; Springtime
Pull-String Bag, page 70; Velvet Blossom Pull-
String Bag, page 73; Cozy Fur Cuff Bucket Bag,
page 85; Beaded Tulle Bag, page 93)

**Cartwright's Sequins
and Vintage Buttons**
11108 North Hwy. 348
Mountainburg, AR 72946
www.ccartwright.com
Vintage buttons
(Buttoned-Up Hobo, page 50)

Duncan Enterprises
5673 East Shields Ave.
Fresno, CA 93727
559-291-4444

800-438-6226
www.duncancrafts.com
Aleene's® Jewel-It® Embellishing Glue
(Mod Print Tote, page 36;
Vintage Rhinestone Purse, page 78;
Pavé Polka-Dot Purse, page 98)

Ghee's
2620 Centenary Blvd.
#2-250
Shreveport, LA 71104
318-226-1701
318-226-1781
www.ghees.com
Handbag hardware

Hanah Silk, Inc.
5155 Myrtle Ave.
Eureka, CA 95503
888-321-4262
Silk hand-dyed ribbon in American
Beauty and Midas Touch
(Monogram Hatbox, page 27;
American Beauty Bag, page 32)

Kate's Paperie
1282 Third Ave.
New York, NY 10021
212-396-3670
800-809-9880
www.katespaperie.com
Handmade papers and gift wraps
(Background papers for all photographs)

**Manny's Millinery
Supply Company**
26 West 38th St.
New York, NY 10018
212-840-2235
Polka-dot hatbox, hackle feathers, feather
hatpin, leather rose
(Hollywood Hatbox, page 24;
Midnight Feather Clutch, page 86;
Fabulous, '40s Hatpin Clutch, page 89;
Blue Rose Clutch, page 109)

M&J Trimming
1008 6th Ave.
New York, NY 10018
212-204-9595
800-965-8746
www.mjtrim.com
Beads; evening bag frames; velvet, satin,
organdy, and grosgrain ribbons; quilted,
embroidered, sequin, and beaded
appliqués; purse handles; sequins; lace,
upholstery, ribbons, and beaded trims;
tassels; silk, ribbon, and sequin flowers;
fur pom-poms; tin star pin; Swarovski
Crystal rhinestones; marabou feather boa.
(Bejeweled Evening Bag, page 12;
Beaded Gingham Bag, page 15;
Summer Day Straw Tote, page 19;
Pink Poodle Purse, page 23;
Hollywood Hatbox, page 24;
Monogram Hatbox, page 27;
Mod Print Tote, page 36;
Tropical Demi, page 42;
Sequin Rose Demi, page 45;
Blue-Boots Tote, page 46;
Swingtime Shoulder Bag, page 56;
Vintage Lace Shoulder Bag, page 59;
Lush Leopard Hatbox, page 60;
Safari Hatbox, page 63;
Urban Cowgirl Saddle Bag, page 64;
Tin Star Saddle Bag, page 65;
Girly Weekender, page 66;
Springtime Pull-String, page 70;
Refined Rhinestone Lipstick Purse, page 77;
Vintage Rhinestone Purse, page 78;
Folk Art Bucket Bag, page 85;
Midnight Feather Clutch, page 86;
Silver Moon Satin Clutch, page 94;
Art Deco Clutch, page 89;
Pavé Polka-Dot Purse, page 98;
Marabou Minibag, page 102;
Satin Handle Boa Bag, page 105;
Mini Travel Valise, page 110)

Acknowledgments

Plaid Enterprises, Inc.
3225 Westech Dr.
Norcross, GA 30092
800-842-4197
www.plaidonline.com
Mod Podge® Gloss-Lustré
(Mini Travel Valise, page 110)

Tape Systems, Inc. (TSI)
460 East Sandford Blvd.
Mt. Vernon, NY 10550
914-668-3700
800-331-6758
www.tapesys.com
Ultimate Bond Super Sticky Tape in
sheets and rolls
(Snow-Flurry Lipstick Purse, page 74)

**Universal Mercantile Exchange,
Inc. (UMX)**
21128 Commerce Point Dr.
Walnut, CA 91789
909-839-0556
800-755-6608
www.umei.com
Handbag hardware accessories and
supplies

Wallies® Paper Cutouts
800-255-2762
www.wallies.com
Brenda Walton Romanza Rose Wallies®
Paper Cutouts
(Romantic Rose Box Purse, page 113)

Thank you to the following companies,
which made such generous contribu-
tions to this book:
M&J Trimming, Tape Systems, Inc., Hot
Off The Press, Inc., Kate's Paperie, Hanah
Silk, Inc., and Wallies®.

I could not have completed this project without the enormous contributions of so many amazingly talented people, which is why I feel compelled to single them out, shower them with praise, and subject them to public embarrassment. That's right, I'm naming names. You all have my undying gratitude.

To my mother and editor, Carol Endler Sterbenz, whose incredible love and support carries me across the finish line every time. Thank you for teaching me that all things are possible and for showing me the glory that is the pom-pom.

To my outstanding photographers: Steven Mays, who is always an absolute joy to work with. This book is a testament to his beautiful, beautiful work. Thank you, Steven, for your enormous efforts, the chocolate croissants, and the show tunes.

Marta and Ben Curry, who have my eternal thanks for schlepping, shooting, reshooting, retouching, re-retouching, and for being willing to be trapped in my apartment for months on end. Thank you for your extraordinary work. I am so proud to call you my friends.

To my book designer, Glee Barre, whose gorgeous work and flexibility regarding last minute changes were so appreciated. And to everyone at Creative Homeowner who had a hand in the creation of this book, I thank you as well.

To my family:
My Dad, who supports me in all my endeavors, and gives me wonderfully sage advice. Thank you for taking the time to run errands for me when no one else was willing to. Thank you to my sister, Gabrielle, for her ever-cheerful and generous spirit; to my brother, Rodney, whose sweetness and generosity touch my heart; and to Jessica, for her friendship and for keeping me laughing. I love you all.

To the Santopadre Family, Vita, Angela, and Cathryn, who made vital contributions to the completion of this project by supplying me with a much-needed sewing machine, great coupons, and terrific handbag ideas. Thanks!

To Esther Gabrielides, who, since the day I met her, has been my biggest fan. Thank you for always going out of your way to help me. I truly appreciate your support and your friendship.

To my new best-friend-by-proxy, Ian Bernard, who has gone WAY above and beyond for someone he just met. Monsieur, I am so touched by your generosity. It will be returned in kind. Thank you.

And last, but certainly not least, I must acknowledge the man who is my rock, my sounding board, proof-reader, delivery guy, personal shopper, and decoupager extraordinaire. The man who keeps me laughing, who helps me keep my sanity, and who never says no to my insane requests (Thank God! Although he does look at me funny): Frank Santopadre. How can I possibly repay the love, kindness, generosity, amazing support, and incredible encouragement you have shown me except to say thank you? Thank You. Thank You. Thank You.

Oik. I owe you a pony.

Index

If you like
The Decorated Bag
take a look at other titles in our Home Arts Series
Knit Style and Glamorous Beaded Jewelry

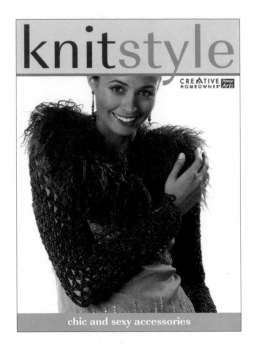

Knit Style is a collection of 25 chic and sexy accessories for every occasion, each original item knitted in today's most popular yarns, like fun fur, chenille, and chunky, and shown in orginal full-color photographs.

- Over 125 beautiful full-color photographs of each gorgeous item, plus instructional illustrations and diagrams of the knitted stitches
- Geared to the beginner and veteran knitter alike, the collection features such fashion favorites as a shrung with faux fur collar and cuffs, a chunky poncho, and a delicate capelet with bell sleeves
- Clear and concise step-by-step patterns and professional knitting tips, together with special sections that show the essential techniques and list the best sources for knitting supplies
- An easel-back, spiral-bound book that allows "hands free" access to the information on each beautifully illustrated page

Knit Style
ISBN: 1-58011-305-2
UPC: 0-78585-11305-7
CH Book # 265142
128 pages, 8" x 10⅞"
$19.95 US / $24.95 CAN

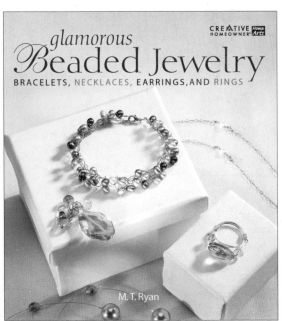

Glamorous Beaded Jewelry presents a stunning collection of 25 fun and sophisticated beaded originals—from bracelets and necklaces to rings and earrings that you can make using an infinite array of gorgeous beads readily available everywhere.

- Over 175 original color photographs of the stunning designs, and easy-to-follow step-by-step directions that guide even the beginner to pieces of jewelry that sparkle with style
- Features chunky bracelets, knotted and bejewelled chokers, chandelier earrings, lariat-style necklaces, crystal rings, and much, much more
- Special sections, including the essential "Beading Basics" and "Sources and Resources," that guarantee near professional-looking results in jewelry-making

Glamorous Beaded Jewelry
ISBN: 1-58011-295-1
UPC: 0-78585-11295-1
CH Book # 265133
144 pages, 8½" x 9½"
$19.95 US / $24.95 CAN

Look for these and other fine **Creative Homeowner** books wherever books are sold.

For more information and to order direct, go to **www.creativehomeowner.com**